Sahar Khalifeh was
entered into a traditional arranged marriage at 18, and
after 13 frustrating years left her husband and decided
to begin writing. The only copy of her first novel was
confiscated by Israeli authorities; her second was
published in Cairo. *Wild Thorns* is her third, and has
been translated into Hebrew and French. Sahar
Khalifeh has two daughters and earns her living teach-
ing at the University of Iowa; she also works for Bir
Zeit University in the West Bank.

Wild Thorns

Sahar Khalifeh

*Translated by Trevor LeGassick
and Elizabeth Fernea*

OLIVE
BRANCH
PRESS
An Imprint of Interlink Publishing Group, Inc.
NEW YORK

First American edition published 1989 by
Olive Branch Press
An imprint of Interlink Publishing Group, Inc.
99 Seventh Avenue
Brooklyn, New York 11215

Originally published in Arabic as *Al-Subar*, 1976
by Galileo Limited, Jerusalem
© Galileo Limited, 1976

First English language edition published by Al Saqi Books, 1985
English translation copyright © 1985 by Salma Khadra Jayyusi

This English translation is published with the co-operation of
PROTA (the Project of Translation from Arabic), Director: Salma
Jayyusi, Cambridge, Massachusetts, U.S.A.

Library of Congress Cataloging-in-Publication Data

Khalīfah, Sahar.
  [Subar. English]
  Wild thorns / Sahar Khalifeh ; translated by Trevor LeGassick
and Elizabeth Fernea. — 1st American ed.
    p.   cm.
  Translation of: al-Subār.
  ISBN 0-940793-25-3 (pbk.)
  I. Title.
PJ7842.H2938S913 1988
892'.736 — dc19
                                                    88-21937
                                                    CIP

Typeset by P.R.G. Graphics Ltd, Surrey.
Printed in Great Britain

The mountain road was steep, and the scent from the arched pines overwhelmed him, reminding him of what to expect beyond the bridge. The pine forests of Jirzim, of al-Tur, of Ramallah. Pine trees, prickly pears, almonds, grapes, figs, olives. Mount Sinai and that 'peaceful land' that had never known peace. No; perhaps it had, once. A land of milk and honey, the 'promised land'.

He remembered something he had once seen painted on the side of a red truck in Jerusalem, a few months after the occupation began. It was a strange picture of two men carrying a bunch of grapes that hung like a slaughtered sheep from a bare branch. And the bunch had indeed been drawn as big as a sheep, each single grape the size of a light bulb. 'Come buy my grapes, as big as light bulbs! Come buy my cucumbers, tender as a baby's fingers!' Yes, a land of milk and honey, truly the promised land.

The taxi drove on beneath the scented green foliage, which stretched as far as the eye could see. The voice on the radio sounded faint, as if coming from the bottom of a deep valley: 'Those sad northern nights!'

Why do these sad songs hurt us so much? Is it because we are a romantic people? He'd never been romantic himself. At least he wasn't any longer, or so he believed. How had he come to that conclusion? Training. Bullets. Crawling on all fours. Pulling in your stomach. Such things make you unromantic in thought and deed. Personal dreams evaporate, the individual becomes a single shot in a fusillade. You can be honed by experience to become a rocket, a guided missile.

That was the logic of it all. They'd said many things and so had we; logical things, historical equations imposed on the individual, making him a single number in the equation. A number. One among others. Thus the equation takes form scientifically, rationally, tangibly. Thus romanticism fades and dreams die. Yes, and poetry dies, along with passion. Everything becomes a link in the chain of the 'cause' itself. But . . .

'Sad northern nights . . .'

The words still sliced into him, into his sensitive, lonely soul.

The car ran smoothly on down the asphalt slopes. The breeze toyed with the driver's *kufiyya*,* making it billow out behind him like a sail. He put up his hand to secure his scarf, then fiddled with the knob on the radio: 'Voice of the Arabs' from Cairo, 'Middle East Broadcast', 'This is London', 'Voice of the Palestine Liberation Organization', 'Israel Broadcasting Service from Jerusalem'. 'Friends, good people of Egypt . . .' The driver spat out an obscenity and glared back at the passengers, at Usama in the rear-view mirror. 'God help you all, how can you bear to look at them?' he demanded. 'They even speak Arabic, the bastards, like they were born to it.'

'They *were* born to it.'

Silence returned. Through the windows he could see the sun's rays spreading over the dark mountainsides, like stretch marks left on women's bellies after they've given birth. The trails twisted and turned, snake-like, as the car sped on down. The fragrant spring breeze carried the mist rising from the lush velvet of the Jordan Valley to the land beyond the river.

* *Kufiyya:* the large square headscarf worn by men in Palestine and many other parts of the Middle East; frequently with red and white or black and white check patterns.

A pot-bellied man with protruding veins in his neck sitting next to Usama held out his hand, displaying an expensive-looking watch.

'Look,' he said, 'I brought this from Kuwait. My sons live like kings out there. Money, prestige, the latest cars. May God continue to bless them! This watch is a present for my son Khalid from his older brother Muhammad. By the way, my name's Abu* Muhammad.'

'Pleased to meet you, Abu Muhammad.'

'Yes, Muhammad's been working in Kuwait ever since the 1948 exodus; then, after '67, Salih followed him, leaving only Zaynab, Hafsa, Hadiyya and Khalid in Jenin. Yes, Khalid's the last of the line. And of the six he's the only one who's been a problem. He got out of prison on bail. They'd tortured him in every part of his body, even down there. They loosed a dog on him that went for his genitals. He may be infertile.'

'You mean impotent.'

'OK, impotent, sterile, it's all the same thing . . . Don't make fun of me. I'm no college man, as you can see.'

'You're fine just as you are, Abu Muhammad.'

'Nice of you to say so. His brothers have really made it; they're men of wealth and position. Khalid's the only no-good drop-out. He helps me in the shop. I try to get some use out of him, but he's a frivolous kid, always disappearing. Every evening before sunset I have to scour the town for him and sometimes I find him, sometimes I don't. He hasn't learned anything, the bastard. You can still see the marks of torture on his body, but he still hasn't learned his lesson. What I'm most afraid of is that he'll do something stupid and then they'll blow up our house.'

The driver sounded his horn in warning and Abu Muhammad regained his self-control and stopped talking. Hiding the watch in the pocket of his loose overcoat, he looked furtively at the other passengers. But no one spoke

* *Abu*: literally 'father of'. Male individuals are often known by the name of their oldest son, prefixed by 'Abu', as here, Abu Muhammad.

until the vegetable farms of the Jordan Valley came into view.

'Do you think they'll make me pay customs duty on the watch?' Abu Muhammad asked.

'Wear it yourself,' said Usama.

'Good idea; but what do I do with the lengths of cloth? Will they charge duty on them too?'

No one answered. They were all wondering what would happen at the bridge. Searches, checks, customs, perhaps even lengthy interrogations, if deemed necessary. Electronic search equipment beeping constantly, and then having to take off your clothes in wooden cubicles, having your shoes and luggage scanned by X-ray machines . . .

Abu Muhammad sighed deeply and muttered some verses from the Koran, calling for patience in times of adversity. Then, turning to his fellow-passenger, he asked, 'What do you do?'

'Nothing.'

'How do you manage?'

'From the sweat I spilt in the oil states. But I didn't make it out there.'

'Success comes from God alone, my son. So, you're like Khalid then.'

Yes, I'm just like Khalid — no money and no prestige. I might well cause a house — or houses — to be blown up, even buses and offices. I'm like Khalid all right, or maybe he's like me. My mother's waiting for me on the other side, ready to stuff me with her cooking as soon as I cross the threshold. I can smell it all already. The steam from the cooking pans, the jasmine in a flower pot; I can see the prayer mat and the beads; I can hear her saying her early morning prayers, before dawn, with the stars still out.

His thoughts carried him over the bridge to the beautiful stretches of the Jordan Valley: al-Fari'a, the green Badan Valley, the little waterfall where people kept bottles of soft drinks cool, the bags of almonds piled up in front of the waterfall, beneath the great walnut trees.

Yes, when will those tender feelings die in me? I've had them all my life! This constant longing for the unknown, this feeling of melancholy that overwhelms me whenever I hear a song or smell a flower, and the sense of elation I feel at sunset. My love and yearning for the very earth of this green land of mine, so blessed and so filled with goodness.

A romantic, right? No way! Not since the training, the shooting, the crawling on all fours; such things make a man unromantic in thought and deed. That's the logic of it. That's the equation.

'Halt!'

The order came from a soldier sitting in front of the wooden walkway. Usama stopped, his heart pounding.

'Open your suitcase!'

The Israeli stretched out his hand and rifled the contents.

'What's this?'

'Librium.'

'Yeah, you people are crazy about that stuff.'

The man's comment annoyed and depressed him. A buzzer on the electronic surveillance equipment sounded and Usama's muscles tensed in an involuntary reflex of self-defence.

'Stand here!' 'Sit over there!' 'Wait in front of the window marked "family reunion programme" for Arabs joining their families.' 'Who put you down for the programme? Your mother? Fine. Come over here. Come inside. Take off your clothes. Strip, strip. Yes, everything. Shoes too.'

A metal prod inserted in the sole of a shoe cracked it open. Usama's eyes widened and his breathing quickened but he checked his anger.

'What's that notebook? Hand it over, let's see if it's really empty. Acid will tell us.'

'Sit down over there on that bench.'

'Usama al-Karmi! Usama al-Karmi! Who's Usama al-Karmi?'

'I am.'

'You are, huh? Why didn't you answer? You were in the toilet? How was it, filthy dirty as usual? Dirty Arabs! We build spotless sweet-smelling toilets and you fill them with shit!'

'Shit here, there and everywhere! You, madam, give me that chain, don't hide it down your bra. Gold isn't allowed. You, sir, what's this? A watch? Who for? Your mother? Will she help pay the duty? Off to customs. And what's this? Material for your mother? Lucky woman, isn't she, with access to all the gold of Saudi Arabia and Kuwait! You all go off to the oil wells and then come back here. What for? What is it you like so much here? You don't know when you're well off. But we do. In a few years we'll be down there and you'll need a permit to visit the Kaaba in Mecca!'

'Boiled sweets and chocolate, forbidden! Honey, forbidden! Absolutely forbidden! It's the law, *Adon*.* Arabs know the law! Over there for interrogation.'

Suddenly, as he made his way along the walkway, a girl screamed. Passing beneath a small window, he heard the short, sharp slaps of a hand on flesh. His hair stood on end and he stopped in his tracks. The girl cried out, 'Swine! You swine! You swine! Aah!'

A short soldier with a black moustache and a bushy beard came toward him carrying a rifle topped with a gleaming bayonet. He smiled politely, and said, in an accent betraying his Iraqi origins, 'Move along, friend, don't be afraid. It's your turn over there.'

Glancing at the little window, the man continued, 'A real dish, but a whore. We found a coded message under her wig. Off you go now, don't be afraid.'

The beating went on, the violent slaps clearly audible through the small window. Usama found himself in such a turmoil of pain and nervous energy that for a moment he lost all sense of where he was. Then suddenly the scream-

---

* *Adon*: the Hebrew equivalent of 'Mr'.

ing stopped and he stood there, listening intently for what would happen next. The soldier shouted angrily at him, all politeness gone, 'Get going! In over there, now!'

He walked forwards feeling weak at the knees, his stomach churning with fear. From his accent, the soldier seemed Polish. He had a blonde moustache, was heavily built and stood almost as tall as the wooden shed itself. A bulldozer could be heard outside, its noise filling the shed. The Pole yelled above the din of the bulldozer, 'What's your name?'

'Usama al-Karmi.'

'Age?'

'Twenty-seven.'

'Where are you coming from?'

'Amman.'

'Where were you before that?'

'In an oil country.'

'Doing what?'

'Working.'

'What kind of work?'

'Translator.'

'Oh, so that's why your English is so good.'

'. . .'

'What's that? Speak up.'

'Nothing.'

'What did you translate?'

'Company documents and correspondence.'

'Who did you work for, a company, radio station or a government?'

'A company.'

'What did you translate?'

'Insurance policies.'

'Oh. This your notebook?'

'Yes.'

'Whose name is this? And whose address?'

'It's the name and address of the shop where my mother buys her vegetables.'

'What's the grocer's name?'

'It's right there in front of you.'

'Haj Abdullah Mubarak, Good Faith Grocery, Saada Street. Why are you carrying this address?'

'So he can direct me to my mother's house.'

'You don't know your mother's address?'

'No.'

'You don't know where your mother lives?'

'No.'

'Why not?'

'I just don't.'

'How come?'

'I left home to work abroad five years ago, three months after the occupation started. We were living in Tulkarm; then my father died and my mother moved to Nablus.'

'Why did your mother move to Shekem?'*

'She likes Nablus.'

'Why does she like Shekem?'

'She's got lots of relatives in Nablus.'

'And why have you left the oil countries to return to Shekem?'

'I'm returning to Nablus because my father died.'

'Who died?'

'My father.'

'When did he die? Speak up!'

'Two years ago.'

'Why are you coming back now and not two years ago? Speak up!'

'I was waiting for permission from the family reunion programme.'

The noise from the bulldozer stopped and the Pole relaxed visibly. He stood behind his small desk, a glass of orange juice in his hand. 'And what are you going to do in Shekem?' he asked.

'I'm going to look for a job in Nablus.'

* *Shekem*: the Hebrew name by which some Israelis refer to Nablus.

13

The shouting and screaming broke out again. The Arab girl was sobbing while a female Israeli soldier yelled, 'Open your legs! Open your legs! I've got to see up there! Open your legs!'

There came the sound of slaps: 'You swine! You swine! Oh! Oh!'

The Pole frowned and wiped his blonde moustache. He started again: 'And what have you been doing since you left?'

Usama kept himself under control and answered wearily, 'I was working for an insurance company. Here are my papers.'

'Where've you travelled over the past five years? To Algeria?'

'Yes.'

'Why Algeria?'

'You charge customs duty on Algeria too?'

'What was that?'

'Nothing.'

'What did you do in Algeria?'

'Nothing.'

'All the way to Algeria for nothing?'

'I just went to see it.'

'What else did you do?'

'Nothing.'

The two men stared hard at each other.

'Where else did you go? Syria?'

'Yes.'

'For how long?'

'Three months.'

'What did you do there?'

'I began work on my Master's degree.'

'Why didn't you finish it?'

'I will later.'

'Hmm. You say you were a translator?'

'Yes.'

'How did you manage to get three months' leave?'

'They fired me.'

'Why?'

'I don't know.'

'You don't know!'

The bulldozer started up again.

'Speak up! Why were you fired?'

Usama's head was throbbing, he could feel the blood pressure rising like a hammer beating on his brain.

'Why were you fired?'

'Because I'm Palestinian, Palestinian,' he shouted angrily.

'Give me another reason.'

'That was the only charge.'

'Didn't they fire you for going to Syria for three months?'

'No, I went to Syria after they fired me.'

'But you also went there before they fired you.'

'Yes.'

'When?'

'A couple of years ago.'

'Why did you go then?'

'To see my mother.'

'But you said your father died two years ago.'

'She came to Syria to see me after he died.'

'So you were in Syria, then?'

'No, I was in the oil countries. She sent me a telegram, so I went to see her.'

'Why Syria?'

'To stay at my uncle's.'

'What does he do?'

'He's got a sweets factory there.'

'Your mother's Syrian?'

'No, Palestinian. My uncle too. And me as well.'

'Why Syria in particular?'

'When my uncle left Jaffa he settled in Syria.'

'Hmm . . . How long were you in Syria?'

'Two months.'

'What about your job?'

'I took leave.'

'For two months?'

'I'd already been working there for two years.'

'What did you do for two months?'

'I comforted my mother and asked her to apply for the family reunion programme for me.'

'Why did you ask her to apply?'

'. . .'

'Why did you ask her to apply for your re-entry? Didn't you like the oil countries?'

'No.'

'Nor the oil princes?'

'No.'

'Who do you like then? Arafat? Habash?'

'. . .'

'Who do you like?'

'Moshe Dayan!'

A smile of derision.

'So you like Moshe Dayan. Why's that?'

'He's a man of war.'

'So you like war then?'

'Don't you?'

'I'll ask the questions! So you spent six months in Syria?'

'Five.'

'Who did you see there?'

'Lots of people.'

Usama smiled wearily, and saw a look of warning in the other man's blue eyes.

The girl began to shout again, her screams mingling with the din of the bulldozer and the shouts of the Israeli woman soldier. Usama walked along quickly, as instructed, feeling as though someone were chasing him with a stick. Then he regained his self-control and slowed down. Afraid? No, I'm not afraid. Then why did I walk so quickly? A simple reflex, nothing more.

He sat down on the long wooden bench and took stock of his surroundings. He was in a large shed. All around him people were sitting in long rows on similar benches. Each carried a number. Soldiers stood at tables piled high with the travellers' clothing and other belongings.

'Usama al-Karmi! Who's Usama al-Karmi? Come and wait over here. Mizrahi will question you.'

'Where've you been?'

'In Amman.'

'Before Amman?'

'In the oil countries.'

'What did you do there?'

'I worked for an insurance company. My father's dead. My uncle's Palestinian and my mother's Palestinian. Me too. I was fired for no reason. They deported a hundred and sixty Palestinians on the same night. They dragged me out of bed. I put a jacket over my pyjamas and they put me on the first plane to Lisbon; from there I took a plane to Beirut, and then went to Damascus. I stayed there for three months and started working on my Master's degree. Isn't that allowed?'

'Sit over here and wait for Captain Moshe.'

'How many times am I supposed to repeat this story? Yes, this is the address of the grocer. Yes, his name is Haj Abdullah Mubarak, Good Faith Grocery, Saada Street. I'm my mother's only child; any crime in that?' You're through with me? Your minds at ease about me? Good! I'll put your minds to rest in a way you can't even imagine!

'This is my permit to go through customs? Which way do I go?'

He stood in a long line in front of the cashier's window. Ahead of him, a fat woman with a thin black veil stood weeping and wailing. 'Ten dinars! That's not fair! Don't you fear God?'

The soldier raised his head from his ledger and waved a piece of paper at her through the bars of the cashier's window. 'Borrow it!' he said.

'Who from? I don't know anyone here.'

She started crying again and clapped her hands together

in distress as though the world was coming to an end.

'Find a way to pay it!' the soldier said coldly.

'That's not fair, Effendi!' she sobbed.

Effendi? 'Effendi!' she called him! Usama almost reached out to slap the woman's black-swathed head. How can you use that word? Why the tears, woman? Ten dinars aren't worth a single tear at their customs counter. Save your tears for catastrophe and defeat! Save them for what's going to keep on happening as long as there are people like you around!

'Be fair, Effendi!'

'It's not a question of fair or unfair. Just hand over the ten dinars and take your things.'

'But it's only some underwear and children's pyjamas. The whole lot's not worth ten dinars.'

'Ten dinars it is.'

'Okay, just take the things, then, and let me go.'

'No way; not until you pay up. Borrow the money.'

'Please Effendi, take five dinars. That's all I have. Then let me go.'

'No, ten. Come on madam, let's get this over with.'

Two Arab men intervened.

'Please, Effendi,' they begged, 'let her take her things. Generosity's a virtue, they say.'

Generosity a virtue, indeed! 'Effendi'! How can you talk like that? What a people! What a people we are!

The girl's voice rose again from the strip-search cubicle, sounding weak now, hoarse and distant, but still audible: 'You swine . . .'

Abu Muhammad whispered in his ear, 'They'll want duty for the watch all right, and for the cloth too. If I'd known, I wouldn't have brought any presents at all. They rob us blind, the bastards. They suck our blood and make our lives hell so we'll emigrate.'

'To think I waited two long years to rejoin my family,' said Usama, 'looking forward to this day as though it were my wedding night.'

'But life inside the occupied territories is unbearable.'

'And I looked forward to it so much!'

'You do remind me of Khalid,' said Abu Muhammad. 'Yes, of all my six, only Khalid's given me any trouble.'

'Hand it over then. Hand it over. Here, ten dinars, twenty, fifty. Come on, please, just let us get on with our job. You, little bride, you'll have to pay fifty. Madam, please don't call me "Effendi". My name's Baruch. Just call me Baruch, without the title. Ten dinars will do you more good than ten "Effendis". Now you, sir, five please.'

A taxi driver took his suitcase, threw it into the boot of a black seven-seater Mercedes and returned to his seat in the shade to wait for the car to fill up with other passengers.

For the first time in five years Usama was returning to the West Bank. The reunion was already quite different from what he'd imagined, quite different from the flights of fancy in which he'd indulged. He felt that the West Bank had now been reduced to the size of a genie's magic bottle. He felt that everything had evaporated: his yearnings and feverish images during five long, barren years of deprivation; the dreams that took him to the bridge every night, and to the land that lay beyond it, to those idyllic green meadows, the clear waterfall tumbling over the bottles of soft drinks in the green valley, the bags of almonds piled up in front of the waterfall, beneath the towering walnut trees. Only hallucinations filled his mind now, and words that droned on with endless monotony . . . oil, Syria, Master's degree, my father's dead, the family reunion programme, Good Faith Grocery, Lisbon, generosity's a virtue, you swine, you swine, you swine.

As he got into the taxi, he glanced around him at the landscape. Yes, heaven was here beneath his feet and before his eyes. But he was now a prisoner in the genie's bottle.

The land around the barracks set up to process entry into the occupied West Bank was grey, devoid of even the smallest shrub. Skilled hands had removed all the natural ground cover of spring to prevent anything undesirable from slipping across the border, to keep out anyone bent on challenging state security. New shoots of mallow had been recently uprooted and their green leaves lay piled on the pavement in front of the barracks, casting soft shadows on the dusty, barren ground.

A soldier emerged from a small wooden sentry-box, surrounded by barbed wire. He yawned, screwed up his eyes with their short, reddish lashes, and held out a hairy freckled arm for the driver's pass.

Having successfully negotiated the check-point, the taxi drove slowly at first and then gathered speed. The wind, rushing in through the front vent, made an irritating whistling noise, but the passengers seemed oblivious to it, silent, lost in their thoughts. Abu Muhammad held out a packet of Kent cigarettes: 'Please take one.'

'Thanks, but no. I don't smoke imperialist cigarettes.'

'But these are Kent. Take one, why not? They're worth it. They took my two cartons, the bastards, leaving me this one packet; they broke open seventeen of the twenty cigarettes inside, thinking they might be stuffed with something other than tobacco. Please. Take one. One for me, one for you and one for Khalid.'

'Khalid smokes American cigarettes?' Usama asked in amazement.

'Israeli ones too. Go on, have one. A packet of Aliya costs 23 qurush now; it used to be 12.'

The driver, listening to the conversation as all drivers do, now volunteered a comment: 'You know what it costs the company to make a pack? Six qurush, friend. The rest is "protective tariff". We pay it and they buy weapons to protect us with. Isn't that something!'

Abu Muhammad nodded in agreement. 'Yes,' he said. 'I smoke El Al now.'

'Israeli cigarettes?' Usama asked, scandalized.

'And I eat Israeli rice, Israeli tahina and Israeli sugar. Commodities lose their nationality as soon as they reach Eliat. And we pay double taxes on everything, first to the nation of origin, then to the new one.'

'And you pay?'

'We pay for what we want and for what we don't want too,' commented the driver, slapping his steering wheel angrily.

Usama glared into the rear-view mirror, staring furiously into the driver's dull eyes. What had happened to these people? Was this what the occupation had done to them? Where was their will to resist, their steadfastness? His disgust erupted into an angry question: 'Where's the resistance then?'

The driver burst out laughing: 'With those who are paid for it.' He then went on to tell a stupid joke: 'I saw a kid once, standing on a wooden crate, smoking a cigarette and chanting:

> I resist, I stand firm,
> On my crate of lemons!'

The driver burst out laughing. One of the passengers in the front seat exploded angrily and launched into a speech passionate enough to move government leaders at one of those conferences that are always being held in Arab capitals. He mouthed the standard clichés, exciting no one but himself, varying the tone of his voice to achieve the greatest emotional impact. He spoke of Arab unity, of how the Arab world stretched from the Atlantic Ocean to the Arabian Gulf. He held forth on the 'tide of revolution', on the Third World nations, on Vietnam . . . oh, how he talked of Vietnam! Then there was a reference to the Algerian war of liberation, the 'war of a million martyrs' as it's called, and to the People's Republic of China, the Opium War, even of the war against house flies. Panting, he concluded, 'And there you sit, like lazy hangers-on, smoking your El-Als and inventing all sorts of justifications for it.'

No one spoke. The driver was smiling; he'd been enjoying watching the man's changing facial expressions. Abu Muhammad sat nodding left and right, his heavy jowls hanging down. The furious passenger spoke again: 'You don't answer! You don't so much as move! All you do is ensure the perpetuation of the species. But it's a species that doesn't deserve to be preserved. You don't think of the future. You're so short-sighted.'

This last phrase stuck in Usama's mind. Yes, the words spoken from the podium by the great leader stirred in his memory: 'The Palestinian organizations are afflicted with short-sightedness.' At the time he'd told himself that it wasn't the Palestinian organizations' fault, but the people inside Israel. Yes, he repeated to himself, it's the Arabs inside who are really to blame.

A woman in the back seat now spoke.

'So! Our friend here's quite an intellectual! Well done!'

The word 'intellectual' clearly annoyed the eloquent passenger, as did the cold sarcasm in her voice. He turned and stared at her, a woman in her forties. Her voice was firm and her gaze steady. She wore a plaster cast on her left forearm.

'You remembered everything perfectly,' she commented, 'except one other thing that someone said.'

'What's that?' he challenged her.

' "Wage real war and we shall be prepared for any sacrifice." '

'We should wage open war? What do you mean "we": Who are we? We're you. And if *you* don't support us, then . . .'

She leaned forward, raised her hand and quickly placed it over his mouth, shaking her head slowly and looking steadily into his eyes: 'Calm down,' she said quietly, looking pointedly at all the other passengers. 'Don't get so excited, my boy. Calm down.'

Usama too tried to calm his thoughts, but failed. That girl's screams still rang in his ears and in every cell of his body . . . 'You swine! You swine!'

'Didn't you hear that girl back there screaming at them?' Usama asked.

'Calm down! Just calm down!'

Usama turned away and stared out of the window. How can you calm down when you're so upset? Anger seemed to boil up everywhere on earth, yet this land they were driving through, his land, was dying from frost. The land itself, the occupation, was a crime we ourselves perpetrated, he thought, and the people's strength is only a myth. We swallowed the rhetoric and believed it was a cause, a revolution. But one hand can't clap on its own, as they say, and I'm alone. I'm alone.

A black-veiled woman implores a soldier's pity for ten dinars, while grown men cackle like hens 'generosity's a virtue, Effendi.' Abu Muhammad sits there smoking his cigarettes from the colonialists, from the occupiers, and bemoans the resistance activities of his youngest son, Khalid. Khalid's one, and I'm one. Each claps alone. An impossibility, while seventy thousand Arab hands are clapping inside Israeli factories! What a people!

The woman spoke again, her tone conciliatory: 'You two young gentlemen must be visitors, not residents.'

Usama, struggling to regain his self-control, replied, 'No, I'm a resident now too. My mother's arranged my re-entry.'

Abu Muhammad and the driver began to talk about the soaring cost of fuel.

Usama clenched his fist and struck his thigh. Turning to the woman, he whispered, his teeth clenched, 'Can't they think of anything except everyday trivialities? Ever since I boarded the taxi in Amman, all I've heard is the panting of the sick.'

'But you also heard a girl screaming.'

'Yes, she was shouting "swine",' he replied sadly, shaking his head. 'And I don't know who she was talking to. Anyhow, you can't clap with one hand.'

Her voice level and devoid of emotion, she asked him, 'Do you see how barren the land is now?'

He looked out of the window. Barren it certainly was.

'There used to be lemon groves here, all the way to the mountains. They burned them.'

'Burned them?'

'They were trying to erase the prints.'

'Prints?'

'Footprints. The trees were on the move. You remember the story of Zarqa al-Yamama,* who said she saw trees approaching with the enemy hiding behind them?'

What nonsense was this woman chattering about? Moving trees? Zarqa al-Yamama . . . Oh! Yes! I get it!

'Well, what about it?'

'The trees don't walk any more, but the prints are still there. Believe it or not, the earth is not really barren and dead. But keep your mouth shut and leave some tracks wherever you go.'

Usama said nothing for the rest of the journey. But when

---

* Zarqa al-Yamama: the legendary Arab Cassandra, who warned the people of her tribe that a hostile forest was advancing against them and was not believed. The forest turned out to be camouflage carried by a hostile tribe, who defeated the fighters of Zarqa al-Yamama's tribe. Her eyes were later put out by her chief.

the taxi stopped and the passengers spilled out onto the pavement in the main square of the commercial centre of town, he looked for the woman to say goodbye. She'd disappeared. A few days later, he saw her among the crowds in the old part of town. Her left forearm was no longer in a plaster cast.

Nothing in the town seemed to have changed. The square looked the same as always; the hands of the clock still moved on slowly and silently, marking the passage of time. Only the trees and plants had grown taller. The soap factory was still there; a damp smell of crushed olive pulp still seeped from behind its huge door. In the main office of the factory the big men of the town still sat talking, but doing nothing. Everybody was out on the pavement, doing things but not talking. Yes, nothing had changed.

There was a pervasive aroma of roasting coffee; great metal trays of *kinafa** were offered for sale on the pavement; the chimneys of the soap factory still belched forth black clouds above the ancient roofs.

An ear-splitting noise came from the radio and television shop. Farid al-Atrash† still moaned his lament: 'You have returned, oh day of my birth, you are back, oh day of pain.' No indeed; nothing had changed.

And yet. The people no longer seemed so poverty-stricken. They dressed fashionably now. And their pace was quicker. They bought things without haggling. There seemed to be a lot of money about. There were more sources of employment and wages had gone up. Prices had

* *Kinafa*: a sweet made of shredded pastry and unsalted cheese.
† Farid al-Atrash: a famous singer of Syrian origin very popular in Egypt and elsewhere in the Middle East.

risen, but people were eating meat, vegetables and fruit voraciously, as though they were starved, stuffing their children. Those who once had not owned so much as a sweater now swaggered about in leather jackets. Those who had not even possessed a scarf now muffled their ears in fur collars. Men's sideburns were longer. And skirts were shorter. Girls who had once been servants now worked in factories and offices. They were plumper, too. Something had changed.

But occupation is still occupation. Dignity excised was still lost. And yet something was different. The servant girls were servants no more, and the class ladder was less steep. Everyone seemed well fed.

Israeli-made goods were stacked in front of the shops, in the showroom windows, even on the pavements. Workers bought things greedily, ate well, dressed well. They stuffed their children.

'Who's this? Not Usama! Come and give me a hug, cousin. I'm so glad to see you safely back.'

Usama threw his arms around his cousin Adil and wept silently.

'What's happened to the country?' he cried. 'What's become of everyone? What's happened to make you so different? What's going on? Even little kids smoke in the streets! I see ads for porno films all over the place, while people stuff themselves with *kinafa* and smile. You're smiling too, Adil. What's become of you all, of the country? They've stuffed you full and made you greedy. They've absorbed you. And I see no sign of shame in your eyes.'

Adil drew a hand across his brow. 'Ah, Usama, I said the same thing when I first arrived from Amman. Don't be so surprised.'

They stood there motionless, silent. A big handcart piled full of boxes and bags of foodstuffs passed between them, separating them momentarily. Still not speaking, they crossed the main boulevard. The street peddlers cried out their wares: 'Fish from Gaza!' 'Oranges from Jaffa!'

'Bananas from Jericho!' The seller of liquorice and carob drinks clashed his cymbals rhythmically. The same old newspaper man shouted: '*Al-Quds! Al-Shaab! Al-Fajr!* Kissinger announces a solution to the crisis!' From the television shop, Farid al-Atrash continued his lament; the juice seller's cymbals clashed rhythmically; people went about their daily business, buying bread, vegetables and fruit.

As they turned off into a narrow street leading to the old part of town, a stench of damp and rot, garbage and decay, assaulted Usama's nostrils. Rotting fruit and vegetables were strewn at the base of the walls and a rusty barrel of fish stood in the middle of the pavement. The cobblestones were littered with muddy bits of paper.

'You *have* changed. Everything's different. Your streets are full of filth.'

'*Our* streets?'

'Ours, yours; the important thing is that you've changed. Is this an occupation or a disintegration?'

The tall man did not reply. He smiled stoically, then looked glum again. Usama pursued him with questions:

'What are you doing now, Adil?'

'I bow my head before life.'

'You bow your head?'

'Yes, and listen to the radio, read the papers, and feed nine mouths and one machine.'

'You mean your father's kidney machine?'

'Yes, and the real one too.'

'Come on, stop beating about the bush. What are you doing about the situation here? What have you done over there, on the inside?'

Adil said nothing.

Usama insisted: 'What are young people like you doing to oppose what goes on inside?'

'The same as what you've done to oppose what's outside.'

Usama stopped and stood staring at his cousin's sunburnt face. Their astonished eyes no longer met.

'You don't mean . . .?'

'And you? You don't mean . . .?'

'Yes, I do.'

'Well, I mean what I said too,' answered Adil.

Usama shook his head in despair. 'Yes, "short-sighted", all right. You're the ones to blame. You're the ones who hold the key to the situation.'

'Say "we", why don't you!'

'Nevertheless!'

'Nevertheless?'

In exasperation, Usama said, 'The picture's perfectly clear, can't you see that?'

Flicking the flies away from his face, Adil replied, 'There's more than one dimension to the picture.'

They walked on together, each contemplating his own dimension, and his own sorrows.

'Mother!'

He flung himself into her welcoming arms. A stream of kisses followed, prayers, cries of welcome, news, questions about health, about what there was to eat.

'It's time you got married, Usama, and there are pretty girls all over town. Your cousin Nuwar's become a lovely young woman. She's tall, and she has beautiful hair. She's at al-Najah College and there's always a stream of young men following her from home to college every day, and you can imagine how angry that makes your uncle Abu Adil. You know what he's like. And he's right, too. He's worried about the family honour.'

'How is my uncle?'

'From bad to worse, I'm afraid, son.'

'And Adil?'

'He bears everybody's burdens. And he's always asking about you.'

'I saw him in the main square. We hugged each other and I cried.'

'You cried? Usama, you didn't even cry when your father died! You cried in front of everyone? What will people say?'

'I was crying for our people, Mother, for our country.'

'The country's just fine, son. Things are all right. They'll get better soon; God will settle everything.'

'At least don't say that Kissinger will settle everything, Mother.'

'Singer? You mean there are still imported sewing machines in the country? Come on, Usama, today all the sewing machines are Israeli-made. My Singer must be the only one left. I hemmed all your nappies on that Singer when you were no bigger than a kitten. But now you've become a lion, a real lion. But how could you have cried in the street, Usama, in front of everyone? Whatever will people say about the son of Haj Sabir al-Karmi? Karmi men don't cry. Did Adil cry as well?'

'No, he didn't. But he was upset; it showed all over his face.'

'He bears everyone's burdens, Adil does. Yes, he carries the troubles of all. He's got nine people hanging around his neck, not to mention the kidney machine. Poor Adil. He's on the go from sun-up to sundown. Your uncle goes from bad to worse, but he doesn't complain. It's true, he shouts more these days and gets angry. God help Um Adil.* The poor man's kidneys just gave out from worry. The occupation's to blame. After the occupation, Abu Adil couldn't hold his head up the way he used to. But he's still fighting; he meets foreign journalists, he talks to them. He attacks the occupation all right.'

'And Adil?'

'Adil's as silent as the sphinx, son, working away day and night. He's got nine people to support, apart from the machine. Nuwar's the family's pride and joy. She's so tall, with such lovely, naturally straight hair. And her skin's as clear as milk. Though I still say she's too thin. It wears her out — the housework, her studies and her father's illness. She can't weigh more than a hundred pounds at most. She takes vitamins, but it doesn't seem to do any good. I keep telling her — and I know what I'm talking about — that one day she'll get married, and having children will make her plump as a duck. But when I say that, she turns up her

---

* Um Adil: 'mother of Adil'. Married women are frequently known by the name of their first-born son, according to this formula.

nose and leaves the room. Girls today don't seem eager for marriage like we were in our day. But when she sees you, my son, everything will change. She's radiant, I tell you, like a chandelier. So tall and slim. And you're ready for marriage now. What do you think?'

'Be patient, Mother, I'm still too young.'

'Young! When your father was your age, he already had five kids. I'll always mourn the ones who died, but those that survived I count as blessings. And you're a blessing too, Usama. God give you many children too, my son.'

'But what about the country, Mother?'

'The country's just fine, son. God will provide. The occupation will end.'

'Who will provide?'

'I told you, God will settle everything. Don't you believe in the power of Almighty God?'

Usama changed the subject: 'I can't get married, Mother. I haven't got a job. And I want to save the little money I have for a rainy day.'

'Just use it to get married, and God will take care of everything.'

'You expect God to solve it all, Mother? Isn't there any other way?'

'Don't blaspheme, Usama, God bless you. Don't you believe in the power of Almighty God?'

'But the country, Mother . . .'

'I told you, everything's fine. And soon God will settle everything. Maybe the foreign journalists who visit your uncle will have some influence on America, and America will tell Israel to withdraw and she will. You see, things are not as hard as you think. Didn't I say God will settle everything soon?'

'Mother! Oh, Mother!'

'Yes, apple of your mother's eye?'

'I'm hungry.'

In the evening they left the small house on Saada Street to

visit the family's ancestral home. It was a large house, a real old-style mansion. There were marble pillars, high vaulted ceilings and an open courtyard paved with huge stones. In the middle of the courtyard was a pool, surrounded by lemon trees and sweet-smelling jasmine. Arabesque plasterwork decorated the walls, stained glass lanterns reflected the light and the antique chests in every room were inlaid with mother-of-pearl. But there was a sense that time had sapped the strength of everything in the house, including the kidneys of the head of the family. There were no servants or family retainers left, they had all gone with the other workers to run the factories of Israel. These days a worker's income rivalled that of the head of the household.

Usama was smothered with kisses and greeted with cries of welcome and was then ushered into the large room where his revered uncle was holding court, surrounded by friends, foreign journalists and French television cameramen. A man from the upper echelons of Palestinian society was saying, 'Employment inside Israel is something that's actually been imposed on our workers. We are not to blame and neither is our social structure. It's the occupation.'

All those present in the great room agreed. The French journalists smiled and sipped their cups of coffee spiced with cardamom.

Slim as a reed, she passed in front of him. She was dressed simply, in trousers and a blouse. Her long, fine hair hung loose about her face; her complexion was clear, milk-white.

'Nuwar!'

At the door of the house she turned, saw him and smiled. 'Usama! Thank God for your safe return! When did you get here?'

'Only today.'

They smiled, each appraising the other.

'Goodness, how you've grown, Nuwar! You were just a little girl when I left. Now you're a grown woman – and

33

reading great big books, I see!'

He reached out for the books and she handed them to him. Apologetically she explained, 'I didn't know you'd come back. I was at al-Najah, at the teacher-training college. I graduate at the end of this year. Then I'll get a job and help Adil support the family. What about you?'

'Same as you. I'll be busy bearing the burdens of the family and the world. Everything's so chaotic here.'

'Totally chaotic,' she agreed, frowning.

'God will settle everything,' he commented sarcastically.

'We'll settle it all ourselves,' she replied evenly.

Usama studied her carefully. 'But life's certainly difficult, don't you agree? Sometimes a person's compelled to bow down, to accept defeat.'

'The strong never bow down,' she replied, looking straight up at him and taking her books back.

'Are you strong, then?' he asked.

'I try to be,' she smiled. 'And you?'

'I try to be, too.'

Pointing to a corner where some leather armchairs were arranged side by side, she suggested, 'Why don't we sit down?'

Glancing towards the reception-room he asked, 'What will my uncle think?'

'My father spends every day like that. Seeing journalists: that's all he likes doing. He enjoys it.'

'Enjoys it?'

'What else? Journalists won't solve the problem, but that doesn't stop him. It makes him feel he's achieving something. His role is to talk. It's all just words.'

'Is that why Adil doesn't sit in on these meetings?'

'Adil,' she commented sadly, 'is excluded from them. Adil . . .' She sighed, then went on: 'Don't ask me about Adil. His situation upsets me very deeply.'

She looked away towards the arched stained-glass windows. Then she regained her self-control. 'How about some coffee?'

'I wouldn't mind, though I've already had some with my

uncle. I wonder where my mother's got to.'

'She's probably upstairs with my mother and our grand-mother. Shall we join them?'

'What about the coffee?'

'We'll drink it up there.'

They went upstairs in silence.

'The house is always dirty,' Nuwar said sadly. 'See?'

She ran her hand lightly along the balustrade and showed him the dust on her finger.

'And to think,' she said, 'that people are still proud of owning big houses like this. It's an outdated way of life, it doesn't work any more. This house needs at least three servants, but it doesn't even have one – except me!'

Usama nodded. 'Yes, the time when everyone had servants is over,' he said. 'Does that bother you?'

'No, it's natural. It's up to us to learn how to look after ourselves. But this house is a disaster. No one seems to feel it except me, though.'

'How about Adil? Doesn't he help you?'

'Adil! He leaves every day before dawn and is never back before nightfall.'

'What does he do?'

'He works on the farm, of course. Though I don't know how he manages. He used to complain about the shortage of workers. But he hasn't complained about that for a couple of months, so I don't know what he's done about the farm. I ask, but he doesn't answer. Father asks too, but he evades the question. He's got thinner and paler recently. But he doesn't complain. He's become as silent as the grave.'

She turned, stopped on the top step and pleaded: 'Usama, I don't know how to say this, but you're the person closest to Adil, at least in age. Could you find out what's the matter with him? I need to know.'

Her voice shook and her thin face flushed. He put out his hand and gave her a fraternal pat on the shoulder.

'I'll try, Nuwar,' he said.

Usama stretched out in his warm bed; when he opened his eyes the moon was still up, a fine full moon. He could hear the cadence of his mother's morning prayers rising and falling. He lay there feigning sleep until she ended her prayers with a greeting to the angels she believed were all around her. 'Peace and the mercy of God be with you,' she said.

Oh Mother, he thought, you're an angel and I'm a lion. But who'll look after you when I die? There's no escaping death. And perhaps there'll be prison, torture, mad dogs. But no matter; there's no alternative. We're dedicated to a cause. When it happens you'll say your son died a martyr. And that he was a true 'lion'.

She turned on the light, her head still covered with her white prayer shawl.

'May God accept your prayers, Mother,' he said.

'Good morning, Usama, I pray God will give you a long and happy life and a lovely bride. Would you like some coffee?'

She brought the coffee and sat on the edge of his bed. Crossing her legs, she started on her usual round of innocent gossip, with tales of all that had happened over the past two years. She told him about her departure from Tulkarm, how she'd said goodbye to her friends in the neighbourhood where she'd lived for over a quarter of a century. There were details too of how Adil had stood by

36

her as though he were her own son. It was Adil who'd rented this house for her, who'd arranged for a truck from Nablus to move her belongings. It was Adil, too, who'd undertaken all the necessary formalities for Usama's return, and who'd asked Haj Abdullah the grocer to look after her.

The grocer often asked after Usama, she said, and wanted to get to know him. 'You should pay him a visit, son. Get acquainted: Haj Abdullah's a respectable man.' He was a person of good taste and great kindness, she went on, even though some people criticized him because he sold cigarettes and cola to the Israeli security forces. What was the poor man to do? How could he refuse to sell to them?

She got onto the subject of work, and then came out with an unexpected suggestion. Why not work on his uncle's farm? The farm needed help, and Adil was like his own brother. And work on a farm wasn't that hard.

'Your father was a farmer all his life,' she reminded him. 'He turned that rocky land into a real paradise. He would dig out those rocks and split them, and level the earth. You'll find it tiring at first, but you'll soon get used to it. And there'll be no one to boss you around. Adil's just like your brother. And eventually Nuwar will inherit her share in the farm and you'll become part owner.'

Usama laughed. 'Mother,' he said, 'you arrange marriages and deaths and plan other people's lives. But when real crises come, you say it's God who'll solve it all!'

'Well, our lives are in God's hands, son, but you know what men are like. And you'll never find anyone prettier or nicer than your cousin Nuwar. Adil's like a brother to you. And it would be better to work on the farm than for strangers. Today there are absolutely no government jobs. And none in UNRWA* either.'

---

* UNRWA: United Nations Relief and Works Agency, which is supposed to aid Palestinians materially.

Usama tried to avoid committing himself. He told her about the burned vineyards in the Jordan Valley and suggested that his uncle's farm might face a similar threat. His mother answered with prayers to ward off evil and voiced the hope that Israel would cease to exist. Then she went on telling him of her dreams for him.

What could he say to her? Should he tell her that he wasn't going to take a job, no matter what she said or dreamed? How could he tell her that his mission required him to be constantly on the move between villages and towns, and that her naive plans for him could never be fulfilled? Should he try to explain that he refused to work on the farm not because he was afraid of soiling those hands of his that had never wielded a pickaxe? Nor because he'd prefer a job more suitable to his class. The fact was that he'd accepted his role as a committed fighter, and his destiny was no longer a matter of personal choice or whim.

He studied his mother's face, shining with happiness at her dreams, and recalled some verses he'd composed during his first year away, when poetry had been his sole means of expression. That was before all passion, all poetry and all personal dreams had died for him. Yes, they'd died, and the figures in the equation had been set, and he'd become a link in the chain of the cause. He repeated those verses to himself as he listened to his mother day-dreaming about the future.

> Mother doesn't read or write.
> Just her thumb print must suffice.

Yes, he thought, my mother signs with her thumb.
'Usama, please go to the farm, just go and have a look.'
'I will, Mother,' he promised.

The road to the farm looked as though it hadn't been used recently. Grass grew wild over the paths. The little building once used as a reception room was locked up. He found his eyes misting over with tears as he called out, 'Is there anybody here?'

There was no reply. He stood in front of the locked cowshed and poked his head through a small broken window. 'Isn't anyone here?'

No one replied. But he heard barking, and soon the old dog was there, rubbing against his legs.

'You still remember me then, Masoud?'

The dog sat looking up at him in a friendly way. Then suddenly it jumped up and ran off towards an elderly figure now approaching.

'What do you want, young man?' the old peasant shouted, shielding his eyes from the sun.

He came forward painfully, his bowed legs dragging along in his heavy boots, his pace slowed by the folds of his threadbare black overcoat.

'Abu Shahada? Don't you recognize me? It's Usama, Abu Shahada. Don't you know who I am?'

The old man spoke with difficulty, his toothless mouth chewing out the syllables: 'Uthama? Uthama who?' he lisped.

Usama held out his hand, the old man didn't respond to the greeting: His poor eyesight seemed to prevent him from seeing the outstretched hand. Patting the man's shrunken shoulders weighed down by his coat, Usama asked, 'Won't you shake hands and say hello?'

The old man finally proffered a withered, veined hand and shook hands in silence.

'Abu Shahada, have you really forgotten me?' Usama spoke reproachfully. 'I'm the son of Haj Sabir and Khadija, Adil's aunt. Don't you remember me?' Then he added quickly, looking around him, 'And speaking of Adil, where is he?'

The old man also looked around: 'How would I know?' he said off-handedly.

Usama's confusion and apprehension increased. 'You don't know where Adil is?' he insisted.

'No,' replied the old peasant curtly, his feeble eyes now fixed on the young man.

What had happened to the world? Why had people changed so much? What had time done? And the occupation! This deserted farm, its owner missing and the old man so unfriendly! Usama came closer.

'Even Masoud remembers me; how could you forget me, Abu Shahada?' he asked sadly. 'You carried me on your back so often when I was a little boy. Many's the time Adil and your son Shahada and I played together behind that shed, under the fig tree. And all those times you chased us with your stick when we pointed the hose into the cow-shed! Have you really forgotten me, Abu Shahada?'

The old man shook his fist in the air. Then he sat down on the fence that surrounded the flower bed.

'Don't be angry with me,' he said. 'I don't remember anything any more. My wife says I'm good for nothing. The old witch, she's forgotten what I was like in my youth, how I could carry a calf on my back and a sack of oranges in each hand! Oh well. That's life, I suppose. God help us all in our old age.'

Usama sat down on the opposite side of the fence. 'You simply don't remember me,' he sighed. 'But Masoud does, isn't that right, Masoud?'

The dog was watching him closely, his eyes shining and his tail thumping on the ground. After a long silence, the old man seemed to rouse himself from a deep slumber.

'Welcome!' he shouted. 'And where's Adil these days?'

'I'm the one who's asking about Adil,' Usama objected, surprised.

'Well, I haven't seen him for a couple of weeks or more.'

'And where are the farmhands? What about them?' Usama demanded.

'They all go off to work in Israel.'

'Your son Shahada too?'

'Yes.'

The old man rolled and lit a cigarette. His cheeks collapsed as he inhaled each breath.

'But why doesn't Shahada work here on the farm?' Usama asked.

'Well, it's better over there,' the old man replied nonchalantly.

'Better over there? In what way is it better over there, old man?'

'Lots of money,' the old man replied. 'And none of that "come here, you son of a bitch" or "get lost, you bastard". Yeah, better over there. Lots of money. Plenty of easy work.'

'What?' Usama asked, amazed.

'Better over there,' the old man repeated. 'Nobody stands over you, making you work like a donkey from morning till night.'

Usama took a deep breath. 'But what about this orchard? Who looks after it now?'

The old man shook his head slowly. He flicked a mosquito from his face and spoke with affection: 'How would I know?'

'Well, who knows then if you don't?' replied Usama. 'You cared for every tree in this orchard as if it was your own son Shahada, and you say you don't know?'

The old man didn't answer. He appeared to be falling asleep.

'Wake up, old man!' cried Usama. 'I said, who looks after this land now?'

The old man looked up at Usama, squinting as if to see him more clearly. 'Is this land ours?' he asked coldly.

'Well, whose is it if not ours?'

'How would I know?' the old man replied, waving his hand back and forth in front of his face.

Usama jumped up and began to pace the path nervously.

What should I say? he asked himself. What should I do? How can I get through to someone like Abu Shahada, so poor, so ignorant, so worn out by time! He stopped pacing and addressed the old man again.

'Who does this land belong to, sir? Whose is it, Haj? Tell me, old man!'

'To the landlord, Effendi, who do you think?' The old man broke out in sudden anger. 'Why are you so angry with me? I'm just a hired hand. I've been here all my life. I don't own any land. I don't own anything. My son Shahada was a hired hand too. And he still is. The land isn't mine or Shahada's, so why should we care about it? Why should we die for it? Don't give me that! Nobody ever came and asked about us when we were nearly dying of starvation. But now, now you come! Why?'

Usama stood there in disbelief at the old man's sudden outburst.

'So you've opened your mouth at last! And you know perfectly well how to think and argue. But you keep pretending you've forgotten who I am. Me, Usama.'

Usama found himself seizing the old man by the collar and shaking him violently. The emaciated old body trembled in his hands like a sack of bran. He stopped himself and eased the old man down to the ground, where he squatted, his head bent.

'Abu Shahada,' he pleaded, 'you haven't forgotten who I am, have you? Say you haven't forgotten who I am.'

The old man didn't raise his head or answer the plea. He felt his chest carefully with his dry old hands and proceeded to rearrange his headscarf which had come loose.

'You haven't forgotten me, Abu Shahada?' said Usama in a low voice.

But the old man didn't reply.

Usama's eyes filled with tears. 'Oh, what's happened to us?' he cried. 'What's happened? I don't understand. I don't understand anything.'

He turned on his heel and tramped out of the orchard. No one saw him off except the aging dog.

Adil walked along the dim street, a man on either side of him. All three were frowning, their eyes half-closed, their muscles doped by sleep. It was still night. The moon and stars shone above the street lamps.

They stood on the pavement with hundreds of other workers. Soon the Egged* buses would arrive to transport them west, to the factories of Tel Aviv. The air was filled with the smell of sleep, bread and cheese. The egg and sandwich seller called out his wares, though there was little demand for them. Most of the men carried their own food, in small baskets or plastic bags that allowed their contents to be easily seen.

A few sat on the curb, resting their heads in their rough, calloused hands, trying to snatch a few last moments of sleep. When the buses and covered trucks arrived, the workers all pushed and shoved to see who would sit for the ride and who would have to stand. Every day the men fought for the seat next to the driver. It was more comfortable there, and its occupant had a better chance of a quiet sleep.

Adil and his two companions climbed into a dimly lit truck, fitted out with benches along each side and two more benches in the middle. Those who stood outnumbered those who sat, and they had to hold onto straps

* Egged: the name of the largest bus company in Israel.

44

fastened to the roof. Those with seats promptly rested their heads on each other's shoulders and fell into a fitful sleep.

Abu Sabir, a man in his sixties, began to hold forth. 'Kids are like locusts,' he said, almost defiantly. He had bitter memories of hunger in times past and of standing in long lines at offices of the charitable associations.

'Kids are like locusts,' he repeated. 'Believe me, they polish off everything in the house, animal or vegetable. I eat like a horse myself, so I can go on working like one. I eat lots of meat, though meat's very expensive these days. If my wife cooks up a pound of meat, that's ten Israeli pounds gone, not to mention the vegetables, rice, cooking fat and fruit.'

Zuhdi stretched. He was a dark-skinned young man with a long moustache. His beard had not seen a razor for three days. 'You know lentils are just as good as meat,' he volunteered.

Abu Sabir stared at him keenly and asked, 'Who said so?'

'My wife Saadiyya heard it on the radio, on Woman's Hour. So she started cooking lentils in all kinds of ways – lentils with stock, lentil soup with carrots and chard, lentils in their pods and out of them. And then *mujaddara*,* oh how we've eaten *mujaddara*! Till it blew us out like balloons. I begged her to ease off, but she didn't take any notice. Just kept on cooking lentils. Finally I had to threaten to divorce her if she didn't keep lentils out of the house for an entire year. So then we were back to food that didn't keep us up all night. How I hate those damned lentils! You know why, Abu Sabir? We couldn't sleep. First one of the kids would let off over here, then another would let off over there. Our lives became one long round of explosions.'

Another man intoned, 'Yes, one long round of explosions! Yes, that's Free Palestine for you!'

Adil burst out laughing, and Abu Sabir began to cough

* *Mujaddara*: a dish made of lentils and rice or cracked wheat; staple food of peasants in Syria, Lebanon, and Palestine.

uncontrollably. But he kept a cigarette in his hand.

'Well,' said Adil, 'whether you live in plenty or deprivation, blessings don't last for ever.'

'Deprivation? We've certainly had enough of that, I can
tell you, professor. These days we workers are beginning to
live like you privileged people always have.'

Adil smiled but didn't reply. Privileged? What privileges? he asked himself. Is what my father's going through
a privilege? An artificial kidney. Blood poisoning. Swelling of the tissues. Skin lesions and slavery to a machine.

Abu Sabir, having recovered from his coughing fit, now
spoke. 'Before the occupation,' he said, 'my boss gave me
135 qurush a day. But life wasn't as expensive then. And
you know me – a master carpenter. Well, after the war I
went back to the boss and he said, "I'll pay you 80 qurush."
I said, "It used to be 135. What's changed? There's still
plenty of work to be done, as God's my witness. Don't
forget we've almost starved in these past few weeks of war."
"Well," he said, "there are plenty of workers looking for
jobs. If you don't like the wages, you can leave." So I did.'

Zuhdi interrupted angrily, 'The bastard! Just like the one
I worked for. Listen to this, Abu Sabir. I worked for two
years for him pressing olives in his olive-oil factory. And
not once was he generous enough to give me a sack of olive
mash. So one day I decided I'd talk straight and just ask. It
was winter, the cold so bitter it could've split a nail in half.
Well, when I asked for the mash, he said I'd have to pay for
it! I was ashamed to beg, so I said okay. When he saw my
sack filled with mash, he said, "Have you weighed it?"
"No", I replied. "Well, go on!" he insisted. The sack
weighed 24 pounds. He said, "Right, 24 pounds at 2
qurush a pound makes 48 qurush." I was so furious I could
hardly speak, but I told him, "Deduct it from my pay." And
at the end of the month he did just that – he deducted 48
qurush from my wages!'

Curses on the mean boss arose from all sides of the truck.

Zuhdi struck his palm with his fist, chortled with malicious glee, and went on, 'But I got my revenge, Abu Sabir. Yes, sir! A couple of weeks ago I met him in the street. He shook me by the hand for the first time ever in Arab history. Then he smiled. "Where are you working now, old chap?" he asked me. Nodding my head west, I replied, "Over there." He turned pale and shouted, "How awful! You ought to be ashamed of yourself."'

A further stream of curses was rained upon the ex-boss. One of the men demanded, 'And then what?'

'Well, I blew him a raspberry such as you've never heard, one that exploded like that bomb in the paper factory. Saadiyya was still cooking lentils then, following the instruction on Woman's Hour!'

This was greeted with loud guffaws from all sides.

Then they arrived, and the men clambered down from the truck, each going his separate way into the sleeping streets of Tel Aviv. The sun still lay below the horizon. The sky was shrouded in mist.

The noise of machinery filled the air with an infernal din. Bulldozers and electric saws roared, cement mixers screeched, axes and hammers thudded and banged relentlessly.

The workers were shouting 'Adil! Adil!' in a loud chorus as they stared at the man stretched out on the ground. Blood gushed from four of his fingers, the red flow sinking into the sandy soil from which the roots of orange trees had recently been torn out.

In discordant unison they continued shouting for Adil.

Zuhdi propped the man against his chest. 'One of you go and get him,' he said urgently.

Up jumped a youth from Gaza, a boy no more than fourteen. He ran to the garage where Adil was perched on the front of a big lorry, its bonnet open and its engine sending out intermittent screeches. 'Adil! Adil!' the boy shouted breathlessly; the mechanic turned, a frown on his grease-spattered face.

'Abu Sabir's cut his fingers off! He's lying out there on the ground! The blood won't stop! We don't know what to do!'

Adil jumped down from his lorry and, leaving the engine running, dashed towards the noise of the electric saw. As he ran he yelled at the boy, 'Which hand is it? Right or left?'

'Right.'

Adil ran faster. The workers were still standing around

the injured man, shouting; people were coming and going in all directions, while Abu Sabir lay there propped against Zuhdi's chest, watching the scene with a blank expression on his face.

'Where's the ambulance?' cried Adil.

'They refused to let him have one.'

'What? I don't believe it!'

'It's true. Abu Sabir doesn't have a work permit, so he's not covered by insurance.'

Adil ran off to the information office. The Jew apologized politely: 'I'm sorry,' he said, shaking his head. 'We can get help only for those who have work permits. It's against regulations. I'm sorry, friend.'

'But the ambulances are just standing there doing nothing.'

'Sorry, friend.'

Adil turned and ran back to the crowd of men. He cleared a path and bent down to raise the injured man's shoulders from the ground: 'Lift him up, Zuhdi,' he said. They carried Abu Sabir towards the garage. Someone opened the rear door of a van. Adil climbed inside and pulled Abu Sabir onto the rubber floor beside him. He took off his own shirt and began tearing it into strips, shouting, 'Come on, let's get moving!'

To the injured man he whispered encouragingly, 'Hold on, Abu Sabir! We'll be in Nablus in less than an hour.'

'Nablus!' cried Abu Sabir in despair, 'I'll bleed to death by then!'

He turned his head away and seemed about to faint. Adil bound up his arm, trying to maintain pressure on the veins and arteries, and then wrapped the hand itself in the remains of his shirt. He sighed as he looked at his watch, then peered out at the traffic lights where the crossroads were clogged with heavy traffic. The streets were crowded, the pavements thronged with people from East and West, Asians, Africans, Europeans and Americans. Different nationalities, different races, different colours. But they all

49

had one nationality here in the Middle East.

With Zuhdi driving, the van sped along, narrowly avoiding a collision with an Egged bus. Furious, the bus driver stuck his head out of the window and shouted, '*Aravim!** Damn Arabs.'

Zuhdi returned the compliment twice over and put his foot down even harder on the accelerator, cursing volubly. Tel Aviv was now beginning to fade from sight, though the high-rise buildings were still visible, the Shalom Tower a reminder of its debt to the Empire State Building. Smoke from the factory chimneys was rising slowly, tinging the blue of the sky with grey.

Adil lit two cigarettes and handed one to Abu Sabir, ordering him to smoke it. The injured man put out his left hand to take it, and began to draw on it. The shock was beginning to subside a little and his senses were coming back to life. He was beginning to take in what had happened. He looked at Adil. 'It's my right hand!' he said. Tears welled up in his eyes. 'I'm done for, Adil.'

He let out a deep sigh and began to imagine himself queuing up outside the charitable association, waiting to receive the monthly hand-out. Five dinars, perhaps? The equivalent of a hundred Israeli pounds? What good would that be? What could you buy with that, apart from bread? And you can't live on bread. Images flashed through his mind, memories of the first months of the occupation. The curfew. His wife doing the rounds of the neighbouring houses carrying an empty bowl to borrow some food. The charitable association. The two bars of soap and the bag of sugar. Tears spilled from his eyes and settled in the creases of his cheeks. 'We're finished, Adil. It's my right hand.' Wiping away his tears, he added, 'You've never known the taste of hunger, my friend. You don't know what it's like to be out of work.'

Adil, gazing out at the cotton fields on both sides of the

* *Aravim*: the Hebrew word for 'Arabs'.

50

road, answered quietly, 'Yes, I do.'

The old farm had been as green as these fields, he thought, the plants grew up to my waist, the banana trees were as tall as the sky. And when the guerrillas hid in Abu al-Hafiz's orange grove, the troops burned the whole orchard down. It would be our turn next, he thought, but our trees died of thirst, not fire. The workers took off and the land died. I was left alone to bind up the wounds of the land and my own wounds as well.

He took a drag on his cigarette, exhaled and said once more, 'I know, all right. I know what it's like to be out of work.'

Abu Sabir shook his head.

'No, Adil,' he said, 'you've never really known the bitterness of fate. When its curse falls on you remorselessly you see death as something you can reach only in your wildest dreams.'

Adil shook his head but said nothing. I know all this too, he thought, both through my father and through my own experience; but mainly through my own experience. My father has such a grip on life, as the past always has on the present, an unshakeable grip, impossible to cast off, like a prison record or the grip of a virus clinging to a healthy cell. The very sap of my body, he thought, is threatened by my father's illness.

'Now don't be angry with me,' Abu Sabir said, touching Adil on the arm, 'but it's the truth, son. No matter what bad luck you have, you're still a Karmi, born to wealth and power. Doors will always open to you, the doors of the rich, the doors of the banks. And the gates of heaven too!'

Adil turned away from the other man's desperate gaze.

'You're wrong,' he said. 'People give only in order to take. Banks are the same. And God too. And I don't have anything left to give. The farm's mortgaged and the family mansion's been left in perpetuity to the whole Karmi clan. All I have is this arm of mine.'

He hurriedly dropped his hand as he remembered Abu

Sabir's injury. He felt ashamed.

'I've nothing left to give,' he muttered once more. 'I'm in the same boat as you. Misfortune's united us and made us equal.'

Abu Sabir, his pain and loss of blood increasing, cried out tearfully, 'It won't stop bleeding. My diabetes won't let the blood clot. If I die, Adil, I entrust my children to you. Let Sabir leave school and work in my place. I wanted him to become a civil servant, to be respected and have a proper salary. But it doesn't matter. Israeli cash is better than starvation. Don't despair, Adil. God exists. Let's talk about something else. Tell me some interesting story, so we can forget, or pretend to.'

'A story?'

'Yes, one about our Arab folk heroes like Abu Zayd al-Hilali or Antar Ibn Shaddad.'*

Adil racked his brains, but couldn't remember any heroic tales. Abu Sabir continued, dreamily, 'The first book I ever read was one I borrowed from Shaikh Radi. He was a man of such eloquence that you could listen to him talk for ever. We used to spend whole evenings listening to his wonderful stories, forgetting ourselves completely. Yes, stories of Abu Zayd and Sayf Ibn Dhi Yazin,* or tales from *The Arabian Nights*. I once asked him where they all came from and he lent me a battered old book with yellowing pages. I polished it off in one evening. Next day I started on another, then another, then another. Then I exchanged Shaikh Radi's stories for those that Sabir'd bring me from the public library. So I read Taha Husain's *Days*,* and the biography of the Prophet Muhammad, and *In the Shade of the Linden Tree*.* I read the translation of *Les*

* Abu Zayd al-Hilali and Antar Ibn Shaddad are famous Arab folk heroes and subjects of many popular tales.

* Sayf Ibn Dhi Yazin is a famous Yemeni folk hero.

* *The Days:* an autobiographical account of the childhood of the great Egyptian writer Taha Husain.

* *In the Shade of the Linden Tree:* M.L. Manfaluti's Arabic translation of the French novel *Sous les Tilleuls,* by Alphonse Karr.

Misérables too. That was a thick book. It took me ten days to finish. Would you believe that in that book the poor and hungry took over the military bastion?'

'You mean the Bastille?'

'Yes, that's it. I'd forgotten what it was called. Do you believe that hunger creates power? I don't. I've tried hunger, but all it did for me was wear me down to a skeleton, weak in body and mind. But Sabir says that the book I read wasn't just a story but real history. I don't believe it, though. Anyway, history's only stories that people invent. Just like Shaikh Radi's tales. I once tried telling stories to the other men, but without success. They laughed at me and refused to believe me. They said my tales were upsetting and frightening. So I stopped.'

The van kept racing ahead the whole time, the road now almost empty except for a handful of civilian cars. After a few minutes' silence, Adil turned to look at the injured man. Abu Sabir's face was the colour of wax and the strips of Adil's shirt wrapped round the wounded hand had turned dark red. Directly beneath the hand the blood was collecting in a pool from which it trickled down towards a crack near the door. Life seemed to be draining out of the man's face.

'Abu Sabir!' Adil cried. 'Are you still with us?'

The man muttered something, opened dim eyes and spoke with difficulty: 'I wish someone would tell me an Abu Zayd story.'

Adil realized it was an old tragedy, that the story happened over and over every day.

'I'm sorry,' he murmured apologetically. 'I wish I could remember one.'

Beating her breast in a frenzy, Um Sabir screamed, 'His right hand? Oh no, I can't stand it!'

She began pacing quickly between kitchen and bathroom, bathroom and bedroom, bedroom and kitchen. In the middle of a room filled with various ill-assorted bits of furniture, she came to a halt and began moaning, 'How will we eat? How will we eat?'

Adil tried to console her. 'God will provide, Um Sabir.'

The woman paid no attention to his words, though she was staring straight at him in uncontrolled terror as she beat her breast: 'We couldn't believe it when he found a job that gave us enough to live on. You've been struck by the evil eye, Abu Sabir! Yes, it's the evil eye all right! Oh Abu Sabir, if only it was my hand and not yours!'

'God will provide, Um Sabir,' Adil repeated, ashamed that he could think of nothing more to say.

She went on moaning: 'What a terrible life, I just can't stand it . . .'

As she wiped her tears, the gold bracelets on her wrists glinted and tinkled. Staring at the gold, she wailed, 'They'll be sold soon. Everything will have to be sold. I used to be afraid of what the Jews would do, I used to be afraid of the curfew. From now on our life's going to be one long curfew.'

She went into the bedroom and put on a black coat over her soiled housecoat, which she tied at the waist with an old nylon stocking, so that its hem was pulled up and couldn't be seen below the coat. Thrusting her feet into a worn pair of shoes, she tied a black scarf around her head. As she left with Adil, she called out instructions to her eldest daughter: 'Be careful the soup doesn't boil over. Cut the bread into small squares and put it in the enamel bowl, just as I told you. Bring the washing in before it rains. If Um Badawi asks after me, tell her to consult her beads and to burn some alum to exorcise the evil eye that's struck your father. And if she has time, ask her to go to the Samaritans* to have an amulet written.'

Abu Sabir spoke up. He'd found some slight consolation. 'Well, I still have a thumb and half a little finger left,' he said. 'It's better than nothing. I'll trust to God for the rest.'

His wife's sombre mood changed; her drooping features revived. 'Don't you worry, Abu Sabir. You're alive, and that's the most important thing. And Sabir's coming along nicely, he'll soon take over from you and ease your burden.'

But what about me? thought Adil. Who'll ease my burden? Nuwar? Nuwar's too young and too beautiful to share the burden of tragedy. Basil? He's not old enough to look after himself. The farm? Burdened by debts. And that damned kidney machine's never satisfied. A mouth as big as the gates of hell sucks up money to keep my father's bones alive. While my revered father continues to sit on his throne in the reception-room surrounded by the notables sipping their coffee and cursing the workers right back to their ancestors. The workers curse them in return, and stick up two fingers in an obscene gesture when they hear all that pompous talk of 'inter-Arab aid for Palestine.'

When he was alone with Adil, Abu Sabir said, 'That wife of mine's a treasure. She does all she can to give me strength and courage through her prayers. And that helps.

* Samaritans: a small sect composed of supposed descendants of the ancient Israelite inhabitants of Samaria, on the West Bank.

It has an effect like morphine. But what I really need are tales of glory. I need someone to tell me some stories that will fire my imagination, make me forget. I just wish someone would tell me a good Abu Zayd story.'

Yes, this was no new tragedy; the same story happened again and again, day after day.

'I'm sorry, Abu Sabir,' Adil apologized, 'I just don't know any.'

Adil went downstairs at a funeral pace. His personal sense of grief and loss had become a sense of collective grief, many-sided, like the tentacles of an octopus. Pitch-black clouds seemed to hover above his head.

Was there any hope of deliverance? The occupation. The land. The ambulance. The grief and panic. Um Sabir's black tragedy. The burning of alum and the evil eye of the envious?

The occupation! The word had so many meanings. Exile: a reality we experience in the heart of the motherland itself. Torture: a topic defined to perfection by the pimps of politics at the United Nations. Sink in the mud, Palestine, kiss the world goodbye!

Adil looked up at the sky; dark clouds were gathering in the west.

'It's going to rain,' he commented dully.

Um Sabir shouted back up the stairs: 'Itaf, bring the washing in!'

They hurried off together down the small streets leading to the centre of town. On the radio Farid al-Atrash was still bewailing the sad day of his birth and Kissinger still prophesied a solution to the problem. The notables gathered at the soap factory were still discussing the technicalities of international politics, while Um Sabir repeated the Throne Verse from the Koran and muttered, 'If only it was his left hand!'

Left hand, right hand, Adil thought, anything in the world would be better than my father's renal colic. Blood poisoning, swelling of the tissues, skin lesions and slavery to a machine. What a life! What a death! A slow death, whose costs even the Arab Bank with all its branches couldn't cover, let alone a farm that's lost its workers. Even Shahada had left. Only the old man and the dog were left on the land. Soon the old man will die, and that will leave the dog. My father's blood will go on mixing with his urine. And me, I'm a slave to the mouths I feed, and to the kidney machine. And Usama searches our eyes for a glimmer of shame. Sink in the mud, Palestine, and kiss the world goodbye.

Usama pushed open the massive gates to the family house and climbed the ancient spiral staircase. The scent of lemon blossom from the open courtyard filled the air. Nuwar was sitting by the pots of jasmine next to the pool. At her side sat a short, slim girl whom he at first thought was a boy.

Nuwar seemed a little disconcerted to see him. She looked down and didn't turn to face him as he approached. Ordinarily Usama would have noticed that she was avoiding him and would simply have assumed that she was busy. But now he was determined to find Adil, even if that meant breaking the rules of good behaviour by disturbing her, so he came nearer. Nuwar got up when he reached them, looking embarrassed. She muttered a greeting with lowered eyes.

Usama noticed that her face and eyes were red. He didn't know what to say. Nuwar gestured towards the girl and said, 'This is my friend Lina. She's Salih's sister.'

Usama said hello to the boyish-looking girl and asked politely about her school and about Salih. The girl replied that he was currently under detention.

'But that's okay,' she said, smiling. 'Prison's for men. You never know when your turn will come.'

Usama wondered bitterly how circumstances could make old friends like Adil and Salih so utterly different from one another. Adil supported the economy of Israel, while his friend Salih languished in its prisons.

He asked Nuwar about Adil, and she replied that he was still at the farm and usually came home after nightfall. His uncle, she said, was at the doctor's for the usual tests. Usama then asked about Basil, her younger brother. She replied that he was in the house and was very keen to see him.

Usama said a polite goodbye to the two girls and went up to the second floor of the old house. From the reception-room he heard the sound of raised voices: his cousin Basil's was among them. Usama intended merely to say hello to Basil and leave, but the younger boy insisted that he stay for a cup of coffee so that he could introduce him to his friends.

Reluctantly Usama agreed, intending to leave immediately after the coffee. But the discussion was a heated one; at first he listened with vague curiosity, but soon he was totally engrossed. One of the boys was speaking in a tone that astonished Usama. It was the first time he'd heard young people discussing issues that never would have occurred to them before the occupation.

Basil's friend was saying heatedly, 'Look, this is the situation. First, at elementary school, we're repressed and tamed. Then, at secondary school, our personalities are crushed. In high school they foist an obsolete curriculum on us and our families begin pressuring us to get the highest grades so we can become doctors and engineers. Once we've actually become doctors and engineers, they demand that we pay them back for the cost of our studies. And our parents don't work their fingers to the bone paying for our education so that we'll return and work for peanuts at home. So the only solution is emigration, which means working in Saudi Arabia, Libya and the Gulf. What's the result of all this? Educated people leave the country, and only workers and peasants remain. And that's exactly what Israel wants to happen. But whether it's workers and peasants or doctors and engineers who stay, our mentality and our activity remain the same. We're humble in spirit, feeble-hearted. Men who work like machines, too scared to say "no" to anything.'

Usama was amazed. Was this, then, the new generation? Then there was hope for the future. It would be among these young people that the spark would be ignited. He sighed contentedly and murmured, 'All's well with the world, after all!'

But then he remembered Adil and the farm and the old man, and his bitterness returned. He said goodbye to Basil and his friends and went to look for Adil. It was getting dark now, but Nuwar was still talking to her friend beside the pool. He heard Salih's name mentioned more than once; Nuwar was crying and blowing her nose. Usama couldn't help wondering whether Salih was the cause of her tears. How well did she know him? Why the tears when the prisons were full of hundreds just like Salih? Was she in love with him? Well, if she was, why not? Nuwar was a young woman, just beginning her life, and Salih was a young man of great renown. Why not? He smiled ironically when he remembered his mother's doomed hopes for himself and Nuwar, and hurried downstairs to the main gate.

Adil had had a couple of drinks, and he felt the ground beginning to sway. And when the ground sways beneath you, everything around you seems to be in motion. You try to hang on to something stable, but even that begins to move. You drown, you sink into the depths, overwhelmed by the trivia of everyday life: like being submerged beneath a mass of seaweed, slimy, viscous and with a taste that makes you sick.

Yes, turn on the radio. Envelop me in legends, in glories of old, and in the worship of heroes. An entire nation's drowning while the radio goes on spewing out songs of hope and fervour, freedom, rebirth, the happiness of man. Happiness or fairy tale? Or auras invisible to the naked eye? Myopic eyes, hearts filled with thousands of regrets, hands shackled by thousands of chains, a kidney that sometimes works and sometimes refuses to work, a man in an auditorium mouthing the glories of Arab nationhood, Um Sabir reciting prayer after prayer. Sink into the mud, oh Palestine of mine, and suffer, my people, the bitterness of recognizing reality and being helpless before it. Abu Sabir's hand spurts blood. Diabetes prevents clotting. The great house is covered in dust. The family glories fade, and the big lie's exposed. Worry makes us all equal.

Usama was waiting in the doorway.

'Adil, please come with me. I want to talk to you.'

The ground was still in motion, Adil found, like everything on it. He tried to concentrate, to figure out why Usama was standing by the door at night, in the cold. His voice was blurred with brandy as he tried to find an excuse. 'Nuwar's waiting for me,' he said, trying to escape.

Usama took his cousin firmly by the arm, insisting that he come.

'But Nuwar's waiting at the door,' insisted Adil. 'And the smile of an angel like my sister gives us all boundless hope in the world, though hope like that's just absurd.'

'Come on, Adil,' Usama insisted.

They walked along the street, past dozens of shops, all shut up. The cool, moist evening air of Nablus cut to the very depths of their lungs. Winter had not yet changed to spring. Mud fouled the deserted paths. People were asleep. The patrol cars a constant reminder that the eye can see but the arm is short. Abu Sabir's hand was bereft of fingers now, thought Adil. Abu Sabir has fallen. Listen to those words. They reverberate. They sound in the ear like a drum beating deep in a valley. They mean more than death, more than occupation. Freedom? What freedom? Further away than *Laylat al-Qadr*,* the night of angelic revelation and peace when the skies are rent apart. Doesn't the Koran say: 'How will you know what the night is? On that night the angels and the holy spirit will come down to earth.' Yes, and the angels will smile. Nuwar smiles too. Smiles at the future, at the unknown, at hope without end. But hope like that's simply absurd. Now here's this eager young man beside me, so cocky with his oil earnings. What does he want?

Usama spoke hesitantly: 'Uh . . . I went to the farm today.' Pause. 'And nobody was there but the old man and the dog.'

So now the battle's beginning, thought Adil. I've been expecting it. It's not a new battle. The tragedy's repeated every day. But maybe he can provide me with an amusing

* *Laylat al-Qadr*: 'night of destiny', the night on which, according to the Koran, the Holy Book was first revealed to the Prophet Muhammad.

tale I can use to distract Abu Sabir and help him forget his tragedy. The battle never ends. Just as faith itself never dies. Faith in what? And what can I do about the seaweed? Nine people live on the money I bring in. And the kidney machine needs a new filter.

He leaned against the wall and began to retch. The stench of alcohol mixed with digestive juices spread in the night air. An old man passed by, feeling for the cobblestones with his stick. Around them everything was dark but for an unsteady beam of light in front of one of the shops. Adil wiped his mouth with his sleeve. He found he was weeping. His tears continued on their silent path. Suddenly he burst out sobbing. 'Okay,' he shouted, 'convince me that what I'm doing isn't part of the struggle, that the fight has fixed ground rules.'

Usama didn't answer. He turned his head to one side to avoid the foul smell. Adil vomited again as he walked along, tottering. 'And who's going to fight the battle of the stomachs?' He was talking to himself. Then he went on: 'You can have my life, Usama, if you can only convince me that freedom means that people who can't defend themselves go hungry. And that there's happiness in hunger. Come on, convince me!'

'So you're working inside, then.'

'I want a woman. I need a woman, a woman somewhere who'll open the door for me and let me express my passion and my bitterness.'

'You've had too much to drink, Adil.'

'No, I haven't. Just a couple of glasses. Maybe three or four, I don't know.'

'How long have things been this bad for you?'

'For days, maybe weeks, even generations. I don't know.'

The old peasant's oft-repeated response, his 'how would I know?', still rang in Usama's ears. He said, 'Yes; you don't know any more than Abu Shahada does. Who does know around here, then?'

Adil looked up into the dark, moonless sky: 'Ask Him!'

'And who'll settle it all?'

'Go and ask my dear aunt, your mother.'

'It's a tragedy. A farce.'

'Yes, it certainly is.'

Angrily, Usama clenched his fist and burst out, 'No, it's not really a farce at all. Here you are getting drunk while a girl in a room in a shed screams "you swine"!'

'Yes, here I am getting drunk while a girl in a shed screams "you swine"! And Abu Sabir lies crucified on a filthy bed. It's a farce, I tell you, a farce!'

'No, it isn't!'

'You're the one who said so. Who says so.'

'This isn't the age of the Messiah, remember.'

'No, it's the age of reptiles.'

'Or doormats.'

'Come on, tell me an Abu Zayd story that I can use to cheer up the injured man.'

'Listen, Adil. Stand here a minute, in front of this café. Now get some coffee down you and listen carefully.'

'Don't try and talk serious stuff. I won't take it in if you do.'

'Come on, just drink up.'

They walked on slowly, the cold, damp Nablus night still cutting deep into their lungs, for winter had not yet given way to spring and the deserted pavements were deep in mud.

'Listen. There are orders to blow up the buses taking the workers into Israel. Be careful. I'm warning you. I've done my duty towards you and eased my conscience.'

'Your conscience!' Adil jeered. 'Your conscience! What about those who get killed or injured? Abu Sabir, for example. Who'll feed their children and clothe their wives? And when the women are widowed, who'll marry them? If they remarry, their new husbands will throw the children out on the street. The boys will end up hanging around alleys smoking.'

'They do that even when their fathers are alive,' retorted Usama, 'so what good are their fathers anyway? They're making a pretty poor job of bringing up the new generation, distorting the glories of the resistance.'

'Glories! Do you measure man only by his deeds of glory? What about his weaknesses? The harshness of his life? The rotten system, the mutual hatred? I've forgotten the hatred, because I've enjoyed the blessings of legend. But Shahada hasn't forgotten. And Shahada left me. Yes, he left me all alone, in spite of the bread and salt we once shared. Do you remember when we were children? How we played under the fig tree? And sprayed the cattle with the hose? How Shahada used to pee in the trough? He still plays that dirty game; he's pissed on the whole farm, and on me too! I never treated him badly. We grew up together. But when my father's kidneys degenerated, I got the colic. And do you know what? Last night I heard my own father making some absolutely ridiculous statements to a visiting journalist. Yes, there he was bemoaning the lost glories of the Arab nation, while the French journalist did his best to console him, telling him similar stories about the history of France. The thousands of Frenchmen who worked in Hitler's armaments factories. Can you believe it? I actually felt rather comforted myself. And today for the first time I laughed in the bus! Zuhdi told a funny story about some advice on Woman's Hour, and then about the bomb that went off in the paper factory. Really funny, isn't it?'

Usama shook his head, muttering, 'It's no use talking to drunks. You're drunk, Adil. Go to bed and sleep it off.'

Adil took a few steps towards the door of his house, then stopped and continued muttering, 'Drunk! Which one of us isn't? Some of us get high on the resistance. Some of us on the glories of warfare. And we get high on kidney pains, yes, they really hurt, even worse than birth pangs. But labour pains are at least followed by a birth. We have kidney pains while you go into labour and then blame us for not giving birth! What are we supposed to give birth to?

Has the sacred River Jordan impregnated us and we haven't given birth? Sink into the mud, oh Palestine of mine, and let the seaweed cover you! Let's say goodbye homeland and finish with it!'

Usama strolled along the narrow muddy streets. The discordant cries of the street peddlers vying with one another assaulted his ears. Meat, fruit and vegetables; the bread seller's cart was piled high with loaves made 'inside', in Israel.

'Fresh bread! Hurry up! Come and get it, folks! Hurry! Fresh bread! One pound a loaf! A loaf for a pound! Only one pound!'

An elderly man with a red fez set firmly on his head passed by. He picked up one of the long loaves, squeezed it and then put it back. The bread seller shouted, 'But it's fresh, sir. I swear it's fresh!'

The man walked away, gesturing, as if to say, 'Fresh indeed! You dare to sell their left-overs here!', and disappeared down an alley.

Usama watched the scene angrily. Even our bread! The idea infuriated him.

A well-dressed young man now approached the bread seller and asked in an aggressive tone, 'Where's it from?'

Upset by the question, the bread seller looked around furtively to see if other potential customers nearby might have heard. 'It's just bread,' he said.

Sensing from the well-dressed young man's expression that an attack was imminent, he repeated defensively, 'Now look, sir, this is just bread. Does even bread have a religion and a race? This is top-quality bread – it's worth its weight in gold!'

The young man picked up a loaf; it was stamped with Hebrew letters. And it was as dry as the trunk of an old olive tree.

'This bread's from inside!' he said angrily. 'And it's stale too! Disgraceful.'

This was clearly not the first time the bread seller had heard this. He responded to the challenge immediately. 'Yes, sir, it's from inside,' he agreed. 'And where else would it be from? It's all from inside, sir. Everything! Why not just move on and let me try and earn my living?'

'What you're doing is a disgrace,' the young man repeated disdainfully.

The repeated insult now brought an angrier, more voluble response. 'A disgrace, is it? They called it disgraceful when I took a job "inside". So I stayed at home like the women, and they called that a disgrace! And here you are in your fashionable trousers and smart shirt, all nicely pressed, telling me it's a disgrace. Look, friend, *we're* not the first to work with them. While we were still wandering the streets of Nablus looking for bread to eat, your kind were running round Tel Aviv looking for companies to award you franchises so you could sell their products. Isn't that true now, sir? Tell me if it's true or not.'

He grabbed a loaf of bread and waved it in the young man's face, flecks of angry spittle landing on the loaves. 'Well, is it true or false?' he shouted. 'Answer me, in the name of your faith, answer!'

The young man was gazing at the peddler dumbfounded, his heart beating fast, his expression shocked and imbecilic. Getting a grip on himself, he suggested defensively, 'Well, couldn't you sell Arab bread?'

The bread seller threw the loaf back onto the cart and began to move off, leaving the young man still holding the loaf he'd first picked up. When the cart had moved a few paces away, the young man followed, still clutching the bread, and shouted, 'Hey, wait, take this back.'

The peddler stretched out a hand and grabbed it. 'Okay,

give it here,' he said fiercely. 'Let someone else buy it. It's clear you're from the upper class. Give it here. Working-class people buy quietly, without making a long song and dance about it.'

He went off, muttering to himself: 'One says the bread's dry. The next says it's stale. The third calls it a disgrace. Everybody gives us a hard time. Why don't they just leave us alone! Come on, now! Fresh bread! Who wants free bread? This bread's almost free. Who's for free bread?'

Some boys crowded around his cart and bought without argument.

Usama walked away. He felt alienated and impotent. Frustration lay thick over everyone, he knew, including Nuwar. Nuwar! Yes! Nuwar was weeping, Nuwar, the family's pride and joy. Tears. Disease. Myopia. And Adil says there's more than one dimension to the picture. What's he talking about? There's only one dimension, one reality, that of defeat and occupation. But is this occupation or disintegration? Are they both the same for my country? It's the people themselves that defeat me more than Israel. Adil, the very backbone of the whole family, he's destroyed too. What's left? Basil and his friends? They're still too young. We'll have to wait a long time for the children to grow up. We'll need the patience of Job. But how can we be sure that every single one of them won't turn out like Adil, their hearts filled with regrets, their wrists bearing shackles that bite deep? All culture gone! All integrity gone! Sink, Palestine . . .

But no, the country won't sink! There'll still be people who believe in the impossible. Man's will is stronger than the impossible. Yes, Neruda, Palestine's in the heart, in the pupil of an eye, in the very essence of life. And these people, in all their ignorance and sorrow, with their bread stamped in Hebrew, they're still my people. Keep on saying it, Shaikh Imam,* keep on saying it. Long live my

* Shaikh Imam: an Egyptian folk singer whose songs of protest are highly popular throughout the Arab world.

people, they alone will solve it. Che Guevara isn't dead, Shaikh Imam. He still lives within me, inside my heart. Palestine's in the heart, Neruda, in the pupil of an eye, in the very essence of life. 'May my right hand wither if I forget you . . .'*

Usama looked at his watch. It was late afternoon. He still had plenty of time. Adil wouldn't be back before nightfall. I'll wander the streets, he thought, buy some vegetables. I'll stop at the grocer's and listen to what people are saying.

Haj Abdullah seemed delighted to see him: 'Why, it's Usama! God be praised! God bless us all! A thousand welcomes, Usama. Thank God you're safely back! How are you, son? How's your mother? I haven't seen her for a couple of days, so I thought to myself, her son must have arrived. Welcome, a thousand welcomes. Do sit down, son. For goodness sake don't sit there near the door, come on inside. Here, take my armchair.'

Usama demurred: 'It's your seat, Haj.'

But the old grocer insisted. 'No, certainly not, it's yours now. That's the least I can do. Please sit down! We want to make you happy. You need rice? Six pounds? Coming right up, my son. Hurry up, Radwan! Give the gentleman six good pounds of rice. Mr Usama's very dear to us. He's from a fine family, you know, a lineage as pure as gold.'

Haj Abdullah prattled on. 'Yes, sir, delighted to serve you! Six pounds of sugar too? Now this smoked fish is really nice, I recommend it highly. Your mother decided not to buy any; you know it's not good for her high blood pressure. But she did ask me to put a pound aside specially for you. Mothers! They've got hearts of gold! Yes, they think of their sons even from their graves. I used to say to my dear late mother, "Hajjeh Zahra, just pray to God to bless your son." And she'd reply: "God give you peace, Abdullah, and blessings with every step you take!" And

---

* The phrase is a quotation from the philosopher Yehuda Halevi.

praise be to God, things haven't gone so badly for me. But now, sir, the inflation! Inflation's a fire roasting the whole country. People who used to buy by the pound now buy by the half. Middle-class people like you are in a terrible fix. Everybody is – except for the workers with jobs "inside", they're the ones with money. See that seedy-looking fellow over there, the one who helps me? Come a little closer so he won't hear.'

Haj Abdullah paused. 'Now him, just listen to this, sir, he isn't satisfied with less than ten pounds a day! Three hundred pounds a month, mind you! And even that's not enough. Every month he wants a rise. He complains about inflation, but does he think he's the only one suffering? I can't make ends meet.'

Haj Abdullah took a deep breath, then started off again. 'But things are still okay, thanks be to God, and to Hajjeh Zahra's grace with God. You know, she died on her prayer mat. Went straight to heaven, of course. Yes, she was purer than Our Lady Mary, may God bless her soul. Now, sir, you'll have some coffee, won't you? You're number one here, you know. This is the finest coffee, it comes from Aden. I've got a big machine for roasting coffee and an electric grinder; I bought them after the occupation. My son Bakr supervises the work there. He's a fine boy, everything you could want him to be. Praise be to God! It's a great help to have good children. And it's all due to the grace of Hajjeh Zahra. The coffee-roasting machine works well, it earns us very good money! Drink up, my son. Radwan, clear away the coffee cups!'

Haj Abdullah sighed deeply. 'Look at him, sir, he's still wet behind the ears, but he's already got plenty of lip! Before the occupation I had three workers, and they worked like clockwork. Now, since the occupation, they've been spoiled, and they haggle with us over every penny. May God never satisfy them! They've got uppity, too, and free with their opinions. Radwan picks me up on everything I say. Three hundred a month and still not satisfied!

He complains of inflation! Is he the only one affected? Aren't we all in the same boat? Anyway, you're most welcome, Usama; you know, my son Aref's about your age. You'd like him. Last year I opened up the coffee-roasting shop for him, then I got him married and told him to put his trust in God. And Rushdi, I'm putting him through medical school. He'll graduate next year, and then he'll really be in the money. That's guaranteed work all right. There's even more disease than misery in this world. And when he graduates he'll treat your mother, God preserve her. Yes, blood pressure's a nasty business, you've got to keep an eye on it. And smoked fish isn't good for it either. But whenever she saw it, she thought of you. Welcome, Usama! It's a real pleasure to see you, at last.'

'Basil!' said Usama. 'Is that you?'

The young man responded with a clear, shy laugh. He came in carrying some books; a friend was waiting for him outside. He shook hands with the two men and sat down on a small chair near the door of Haj Abdullah's shop.

'How are your studies going, Basil?'

'Oh, not too bad. How do you find things here?'

'Not too bad.'

Palestine's in the heart, Neruda!

Haj Abdullah asked, 'How's your father today, Basil? Better, God willing?'

'He's okay.' The young man drank greedily from a bottle of cola, then turned to the grocer and asked, 'Where's Hani?'

Haj Abdullah didn't answer, but said instead, 'Hani's my youngest son. I'll introduce him to you soon, Mr Usama. He's a real rascal, I tell you, a regular firebrand. How are your studies going, Basil? Or is politics taking up all your time? Mr Usama, sir, I must complain to you about these boys. Every day they stand round the door of my shop talking endlessly about politics. They go from Dayan to Eshkol to Golda Meir to Sadat to Arafat right on into the night. I remind them about their studies, but they say everything's okay; when I ask about their grades they say it's okay, or about the police patrols, and they say it's okay. I don't know! They're a generation only God can control.'

He took another deep breath and then continued: 'Come closer so no one will hear. I'm afraid, Mr Usama, that these boys might get involved in something. Then we'll have to go begging to the mayor and the Red Cross. You know how many are in prison? They go in fit and strong and they come out thin as reeds. You've no idea! The patrol cars keep coming and going and we're afraid for them all the time.'

'Let them talk, Haj Abdullah, let them think.'

'But I'm afraid they'll do something, Mr Usama. Really. Hani's crazy. I can't control him at all. Every time I tell him to be sensible, he says everything's okay. I don't know where it'll all end. Tell me, what's the news abroad? Should we believe the broadcasts or what we can see for ourselves? I mean, will there be war? Is it likely the Arabs will be able to get themselves together and go to war?'

Haj Abdullah sighed. He leaned forward. 'Once,' he said, 'one of the patrols told me: "We'll soon be in Aswan." And your cousin Basil just wouldn't keep quiet. No. He opened his mouth and the words simply spewed out. He let rip and so did Hani. And the Jew left the shop with his eyes blazing. Ever since then the patrol cars come by all the time. Your cousin sits there in the shop holding forth, while Hani listens. I'm afraid they're going to start something, and then we'll be in one hell of a mess. A hand can't fight an awl, can it, Mr Usama? That's right, isn't it?'

'Let them talk, Haj Abdullah. Let them think.'

'Just talk, my son? But where will it lead? What good will it do? We've been trading in words for twenty-five years. And that's a business guaranteed to fail one hundred per cent. Better be in the smoked fish trade than in the word racket.'

'But we don't just talk,' Basil burst out angrily.

The other two stared at him. He went red, and then

covered his embarrassment with a boyish laugh.

'We . . . we study too,' he said.

The three of them smiled. Usama picked up the things he'd bought and set off home.

In the evening Usama went out to look for Adil. He waited near the town hall where the workers' buses unloaded. Adil soon stepped down, dressed in his work clothes and accompanied by a man with very broad shoulders. When he saw Usama, Adil frowned.

'This is Zuhdi, who works with me,' he said. 'Zuhdi, meet my cousin Usama.'

Having made the introductions, Adil lapsed into silence, leaving Zuhdi to pick up the conversation. 'Well now, welcome home; glad to see you safely back,' he offered. 'What's new outside? Tell me: will the Arabs fight or not? If things go on here the way they are now, I'm getting out.'

'Where to, Zuhdi?'

'Kuwait, Bahrain, Australia – it makes no difference.'

'You shouldn't say that. This is our country. The occupation's going to end soon, and we'll be free.'

'Rubbish, my friend, rubbish,' answered Zuhdi. 'The radio broadcasts will take care of everything, you mean? No more wars or anything else; are you kidding? How long are we going to put up with this lousy situation? I've had it up to here; up to here, I tell you. We can't please our own people, or those bastards over there either. I swear by God Almighty, if it weren't for my kids I'd take off for Syria and come back with a machine-gun. The eye can see but the arm is short – don't you agree, Adil?'

'Come on, hurry up,' Adil replied irritably. 'Abu Sabir's

waiting, remember. Yesterday we promised we'd visit him.'

The three men walked on in silence, deep into the back streets of the old town. They passed Haj Abdallah's shop, where the boys were holding their usual evening meeting, discussing politics. Hani, occupying his father's chair, shouted, 'Come on in everyone. Have some coffee or a soft drink.'

Zuhdi laughed and made a ribald comment that set the boys giggling. Adil, still frowning, raised a hand in greeting. Usama smiled and promised the boys he'd come to one of their meetings, but not just then. As they walked on, Zuhdi talked and Usama listened; Adil simply plodded ahead, silent and distracted.

'Yes, there's hardly a job I haven't tried my hand at,' Zuhdi was saying. 'Mechanic, electrician, builder, porter, waiter – everything you can think of. And I've emigrated more than once – to Kuwait, Dhahran, Germany. I wasted a lot of sweat in German factories, I can tell you. But there I felt no difference between me and any other worker. Here there's a big difference between Muhammad and Cohen: Muhammad gets the heavy work, Cohen the light. The Jewish workers have cafeterias with tables and chairs, but we sit on the ground to eat, in the sun or in the garage with the scrap metal and the oil and grease. Isn't that right, Adil?'

Adil didn't answer. Whatever pain he was feeling was etching deep furrows on his face. Usama, watching out of the corner of his eye, felt ashamed and looked down.

As Zuhdi spoke, he made sweeping gestures with his hands: 'I agree with Abu Sabir, God help him! Children are like locusts. They devour everything, ripe or unripe, juicy or dry. He's right. A couple of days ago I put a whole chicken in front of my two kids and they polished off the whole thing. She's five and he's four! They ate everything, meat, wings and skin, then sucked the bones. Who'm I working for, I ask you? Last night we had sheep's head and tripe. The bowl was filled to overflowing. Bread, rice and sauce as well as the head and the tripe. Cost an arm and a leg. You need so many things to live these days. The prices burn us up like hellfire. And apart from the meat, there's bread, vegetables, fruit, water, electricity and everything else.'

They walked on. Zuhdi kept the conversation going: 'When I came back from Kuwait,' he explained, 'I worked in an olive-oil factory. The owner exploited me because unemployment was so high. I was disgusted. I left there swearing I'd rather die of hunger than go back. Then I worked as a taxi driver on the Rafidiyya line. That was okay, but then the bastards took away my licence. For no reason. So there I was sitting at home, like a woman. One day I was sitting brooding in the café, and I had just seventy piastres in my pocket. Abu Nawwaf told me about a job as a driver for some company. I thought about it, and I said to myself: "Now Zuhdi, you're a family man, so instead of emigrating again, stay here in your own country and share everyone else's plight. That's better than going abroad. Exile's tough, old friend. You know what exile's like!" I'd wandered from country to country to earn forty-five Kuwaiti dinars – thirty-four Jordanian. Work it out for yourself. I was living with four others in a room like a prison cell. And when the hot sandstorms, the *touz,* blew up we suffered absolute agony. What can I say? Exile's bitter, that's all there is to it. So I said to myself: "Zuhdi, why go into exile? It's better to stay at home." So I said to Abu Nawwaf: "Is it a black-market job, or *lishka** post?"'

'*Lishka*?' Usama asked.

'Yes, my friend. *Lishka* means a job arranged through the employment office. You don't know about that? *Lishka* jobs have security. If Abu Sabir'd had a *lishka* job, he'd have got compensation.'

---

* *Lishka*: literally 'office' in Hebrew; here a colloquial designation of *lishkat avoda,* or 'employment office' for officially recognized jobs.

'Abu Sabir?'

'You don't know about Abu Sabir? You'll be seeing him in a minute. His fingers flew off before the blade of his saw, one after the other, like sardines running from danger.'

Usama imagined the scene as vividly as if he'd witnessed it himself. He turned aside feeling nauseated. When he turned back to the others, Adil was looking at him with disgust.

All right, I know what you're thinking, Usama said to himself, I know. You think I'm bourgeois. God, how things change! You'll soon be taunting me about my well-pressed trousers and shirt, just like the bread seller. Is this what you call 'class defection'? No, class defection is just a state of mind. But in Adil's case his own status has dropped, and how low it's sunk!

In his imagination, Usama could still see Abu Sabir's fingers flying; he felt his own blood flowing, cold and sticky. A shocking idea suddenly struck him. Would he be able to undertake the mission that was required of him? How could he actually kill people – he, Usama, who'd once mourned for a lamb slaughtered on a feast day?

He remembered that day well. They'd been living in Tulkarm then, and their father had bought the family a lamb as white as snow. Usama used to take it in his arms, and feed and play with it as if it were a child. When he stood it before the wardrobe mirror, the little lamb had thought its reflection was that of a rival and had retreated a few steps before charging; if its horns had been any bigger than two bumps the size of mulberries, the mirror would have been smashed and his mother would have raised hell. But it was tiny, the lamb, a fat little ram no bigger than Zuhdi's lunch basket. Yes, its wool was as white as snow. They'd sacrificed it for the feast. Usama had wept and refused to eat. He'd eulogized the lamb in a poem that the family had joked about for weeks. And at the time no one had really understood Usama's poem except his cousin Adil. How times change, he thought bitterly.

Zuhdi was talking again: 'Yes, they refused him first aid, would you believe it? Because his job wasn't *lishka*. Abu Sabir had tried to avoid paying taxes for the "social security" we never benefit from, for union fees, and for "national insurance".'

'National insurance?'

'Yes, my friend. "National insurance" is to defend you in time of war. And the tax is a "liberation tax", don't you see? You're now in the "liberated territories". Didn't you hear Radio Israel announce that in '67? Yes, you've been liberated, my friend. And if you don't believe it, just you ask the *Adons*.'

'*Adons*?'

'Yes, of course. Oh, but I'm forgetting you don't know about all that. You're still at the very beginning of your experience of "liberation". You'll soon learn – words like *Adon*, and *giveret*, and *islakhli*, and *shalom*.* Those words, my friend, mean that the person's educated and polite. As for *Aravim*, that means you're a rotten thief, a pig and the son of a pimp. The last time I heard that word was from an Egged driver. I cursed his mother and his father too. But he didn't hear what I said, or understand. Anyway, I relieved my own feelings. Words are our only weapon, my friend. It's a rotten situation, but the pay's secure. They take the ground from under your feet, then call you "friend". They're bastards, they only show you some respect if they need the labour of your strong arms. And when you can't work any more, they won't lower themselves to return your greeting. But the situation in Kuwait was very bad too. Better the bitter herb of your own people than the honey of your enemy, though, as the saying goes. What do you think? What should I do? Shall I take off for Germany or Kuwait or stay here? What do you say, sir? I'm asking whether I should leave the country or stay here.'

* *Giveret:* the word used for 'madam'. *Islakhli:* 'excuse me' in Hebrew. *Shalom:* literally 'peace', the standard greeting.

Usama was perplexed. 'You're asking me?'

'Yes, I'm asking you, sir. Who else would I be talking to? You didn't hear what I was saying, right? Never mind. You're not the first. Don't give it a thought. We're used to speaking while people nod their heads without listening. Forget it. Here's the door. Please, after you. No, no, after you, I insist. Oh no, I couldn't go first – you're our guest. After you!'

Usama pushed open the creaking wooden door and they found themselves in a small, paved courtyard. In front of the steps stood a bucket of rubbish from which oozed a black liquid. A little girl of about four sat on the filthy ground to the right of the bucket, holding a scrap of faded cloth. This she dipped into an open drain with soap suds floating on its surface. She was pressing and wringing out the cloth with both hands, in imitation of grown women.

She looked up at the three men, her gaze resting on Usama. Her long stare surprised him and made him ill at ease. He tried to cover his embarrassment by gazing around him; filth and poverty were apparent everywhere. His nose was filled with the stench of decomposition and decay. He felt depressed and nauseated. The girl was still staring fixedly at him.

Was this the gaze of a child? Why do children lose their innocence? Why is she hostile to me? It's as if she knows!

Adil went over to her, tweaked her tanned cheek and handed her a piece of coconut. She took it without smiling. She wasn't pretty, not even nice-looking. Adil smiled as he asked her, 'Where are your brothers?'

Without removing her eyes from Usama, she frowned and replied, 'Outside. In the street.'

They climbed the stairs and stopped at the door at the very top. Zuhdi called out, 'Abu Sabir!' A woman in her forties looked out. She was overweight, her face discoloured. On her wrists she wore gold bracelets weighing at least half a pound.

She greeted them effusively, enunciating, in a harsh voice, a stream of pious formulas and welcoming phrases. And there, amidst the chaos of the family's belongings, lay Abu Sabir, stretched out on an iron bed. He seemed buried beneath piles of covers, but his injured hand lay on top. He lifted his head and tried to raise his body. Adil hurried over and helped him lie down again, speaking to him in a near whisper.

The woman continued her welcomes; they each sat on a chair. Abu Sabir asked for another pillow and his wife placed it under his head. He began bidding his visitors welcome.

'This is my cousin Usama,' explained Adil. 'He came along to see how you are.'

'Welcome! Welcome! I'm most honoured by your visit. You shouldn't have put yourself out, sir.'

The conversation went back and forth, centring on compensation for unemployment and for the injury Abu Sabir had suffered. Adil was clearly deeply involved in the issue, and kept insisting that compensation was a legal right that had to be demanded despite the lack of a work permit. The subject was discussed at great length, and Usama became increasingly depressed as he watched his cousin.

Obviously it would not be easy to convince Adil to abandon this present position to which he seemed so enthusiastically committed. All this talk of *lishka, shalom* and *islakhli*. What a civilization; what a mess! Stop all this, Adil, and raise your head, he thought. Get rid of all this disease and dust. Clear your vision. There's more than one dimension to the picture, even with defeat and occupation. Was what was happening occupation or disintegration? The two seemed the same. My own people defeat me more than Israel. The patience of Job indeed! Are we supposed to endure until the children grow up? Che Guevara isn't dead, Shaikh Imam! He's still here, in this heart of mine. Palestine's in the heart, Neruda! In the pupil of an eye, in the very essence of life. Our nation will never sink. There'll always be people who believe in the impossible.

Abu Sabir suddenly asked him, 'What's new outside? Will there be war or not? Set my mind at rest.'

Usama drew a deep breath, preparing himself for a difficult campaign of consciousness-raising.

'It all depends on the people inside.'

Abu Sabir and Adil exchanged looks. Usama noticed and his face flushed. He repeated sharply, 'The people outside insist that everything depends on those inside.'

Abu Sabir stretched out his good arm and touched Adil's hand: 'Tell him, Adil.'

Adil puffed silently on his cigarette.

Zuhdi complained loudly: 'Speak plainly, can't you, man? Tell us straight out, is it war or not?'

Usama repeated stubbornly, 'It all depends on the people inside.'

Zuhdi made a gesture of impatience.

'Don't worry,' said Usama. 'There'll be a war . . . But no one can say exactly when.'

Zuhdi shouted angrily, 'Come on. Tell us when. When, for heaven's sake? It's been five damned years, for God's sake! I swear the *touz* of Kuwait, hellish though they were, were better than things are here now. If the situation continues for another six or seven months, I tell you, I'm not staying in this country, no way!'

He glanced at Adil, lowered his voice a little, and said somewhat less angrily, 'It's true that the country belongs to those who live here, but there are limits to patience, folks.'

He glanced around, seeking encouragement. But when he found none, he looked at Adil again, apologetic now. 'Well, it's true that I'm not in such a bad way as some people. But to hear them denigrate us Arabs every morning, and shout *Aravim*!, makes you lose all faith in your own people. There are limits to patience, after all. One day there's talk of Gunnar Jarring, the next it's Kissinger and then the next it's Azrail the angel of death, until you're ready to give up the ghost yourself. Here we are, burying our own shit all the time, and along comes Mr Usama to tell us we've got to rely on ourselves. Tell him, Adil, by your father's life, tell him! Tell him how the people inside are suffering. Tell him how Israel's blown up twenty thousand homes and four whole villages. Tell him how the detention camps are as full of young men as a cheap public bath's full of cockroaches. Tell him what happened to al-Bahsh's son and to al-Shakhshir and al-Huwari's daughters.* But the worst thing is that all of us, every last one of us, are forced to work in their brothels just in order to live!'

Usama stood up abruptly: 'Goodbye all!' he said.

Adil didn't move. Zuhdi got up and put out his hand: 'Where are you off to, my grumpy sir? Why such a rush? We haven't finished.'

Abu Sabir grasped Adil by the arm: 'Bring him back, Adil. It's not right: the man hasn't had any coffee yet.'

'It doesn't matter,' Adil replied with a calm he didn't feel.

'This is your fault, Zuhdi,' scolded Abu Sabir. 'You made him angry.'

'No, that's not true,' said Adil. 'Zuhdi only spoke the truth.'

'Well, why did he get so upset?'

'He just doesn't want to hear it.'

Abu Sabir smiled wanly: 'I get it. He only wants to hear nice Abu Zayd stories.'

Adil stood up: 'And I've told him in all sincerity that I don't know any.'

Usama was gone, but Zuhdi still brooded over the way Usama had humiliated him. 'I'm an ass,' he was saying, 'an ass and the son of an ass. All the way here I was talking and he just nodded his head. But when I asked him one little question, it was obvious he hadn't been listening. I

---

* The reference is to three young people brutally tortured by Israeli soldiers in a demonstration against the occupation.

thought he was like you, brother Adil. But it's clear this cousin of yours wants to impose his own ideas on us. Well, we're having none of it. Tell him we've reached the end of the road. Tell him we don't need it. This is what always happens,' he went on angrily, banging the cane chair with his hand. 'We speak, but they don't hear us. Who can we speak to? For God's sake, who can we speak to?'

The weeks passed and Usama accomplished none of his objectives. There was no way he could get through to Adil, nor could he carry out any secret missions. Two mutually antagonistic factors were at work within him. Although he believed unequivocally that all the Egged buses had to be blown up and that the workers had to abandon their treacherous role, Adil's unexpected presence among them created a cruel dilemma. Usama did his best to convince himself that Adil was only one of thousands and that the possibility of his being a victim of the planned operations was only one element in the greater scheme of sacrifice for which he, Usama, had accepted responsibility. He was committed, after all, and emotions, of whatever kind, had to be suppressed. So what if Adil died? Or ten like him? The individual was of no importance when the fate of the community was at stake. And Adil himself was only one individual.

But having reached this conclusion, Usama would then remember their childhood together and the part Adil had played in his own upbringing and education. He'd learned so much from Adil; they'd spent long hours together, discussing the future and enjoying a host of intellectual adventures. They'd dreamed of playing the kind of role the Rothschilds had done. Since money, they said to each other, was the only language the West understood, they'd address the West in terms of cash and capital. No. No, that wasn't true. That had actually been the one difference of opinion between Adil and himself. Economics didn't determine history, Usama had always insisted. Materialism wasn't the motivating force; it was neither the incentive nor the objective. What about principles, ethics and values? What about truth and justice? In spite of their wide differences, they'd always agreed on one point: the value of the individual existed only through the group. Today, the difference between them lay in the fact that each believed he was in accord with the group. Usama shook his head in regret. If Adil had only left the West Bank and met with comrades elsewhere, he'd have understood what was necessary. The area where they now stood, bounded by the river on one side and enemy fortifications on the other, had become a major threat to revolutionary thought in the whole region. For the people had become soft, been brain-washed with lies and Israeli cash.

His own duty was to accomplish his mission, no matter what the sacrifices. Adil, he told himself, was totally deluded, his shameful position couldn't be justified on any grounds. Nine mouths to feed? People weren't going to die of starvation. The kidney machine? To hell with it! It was better for a sick person to die than to go on living. The services Adil had performed for Usama's mother during his absence were a duty dictated by family ties and respon-sibilities. These were debts that Usama himself would be able to repay in time – he was still young, after all. And even if his own life were to end one way or another (which was quite possible), his mother wouldn't die of starvation. No, not even if his uncle and Adil were both to die. The comrades abroad would take care of things. People here would understand. Even if the older generation didn't, the younger ones would understand when they grew up.

Usama came to a stop before the café where the workers gathered in the evening; he couldn't resist the temptation to go in. He wanted to see Adil one last time. He shook his head sadly. Every time he saw Adil he promised himself it would be the last, that it wouldn't hurt to have one last try at converting him to the cause. Adil was a young man of unblemished reputation. Had it not been for his recent change of heart, his intellectual and physical powers could have been put to good use. Adil was an obvious candidate for an active leadership role; he possessed all the necessary qualities. In his current position, with his popularity among the workers, he could influence scores, perhaps even hundreds, of people. If only he could convince Adil. When he remembered his discussions with Basil's young friends, he felt more optimistic. Perhaps, after all, he would be able to influence Adil, just as he had the boys. But Adil refused to listen to him. 'There's more than one dimension to the picture,' he'd say. And that was what lay at the heart of the problem between them. Usama firmly believed that there was no longer more than one dimension to the issue, not after the 1967 defeat and the occupation that followed.

He sat down at the far end of the café; the table was strewn with coffee cups, tea glasses and a backgammon board. The formica surface was so scratched and stained that it was difficult to tell what its original colour might have been.

Usama found the noise deafening. The click of the back-gammon pieces and the slap of the dice set his frayed nerves on edge. Clouds of cheap cigarette smoke billowed out of the mouth of a peasant sitting nearby. Usama thought of his meeting with Abu Shahada; he still felt angry and bitter when he remembered the details of their conversation. These men have no loyalty to past relation-ships, he thought, to the bread and salt they once shared; they just want whatever everyone else has. Like the detest-able bread seller, making fun of well-ironed shirts and trousers. Or Abu Sabir's wife, with gold bangles on her wrists. And Zuhdi, whose comments reflected only conceit and ignorance. What did they expect, to live lives of luxury under the occupation? Was that their concept of patriotism and nationalism? That damned Zuhdi knew perfectly well that the word *Aravim* also implied 'dirty thief', 'pig' and 'son of a pimp'. Yet he still worked inside and pretended to defend himself with strings of curses. The only threat he could think of was to emigrate! What stupidity! Zuhdi and Shahada and their like needed to be taught a lesson they'd never forget. And Abu Sabir . . . A dismal image rose to the surface of his mind, a memory of the face of a little girl playing with a filthy rag beside a bucket of rubbish. Why did children lose their innocence? He shuddered when he remembered that her eyes had not been those of a little girl at all, that her gaze had seemed to bore into his head and read his thoughts, thoughts that threatened her father and everyone like him.

Engulfed by a rising sense of panic, Usama nodded to the waiter. 'It's my nerves,' he thought. They felt worn to a frazzle. He wasn't seeing clearly any more. Attaching fantastic interpretations to a little girl's stare! A child!

The acrid tobacco smoke was giving him a headache. A peasant was puffing away near him and another man's voice seemed deafeningly loud.

'Every morning our heads are heavy with sleep,' the man was saying. 'Good health is like wages – it varies from day to day. And it's not the Jews we fear most. What we're really scared of is getting sick or disabled and losing our jobs. City people just don't realize the meaning of the words: "he croaked." It reverberates in the brain like a drumbeat, more threatening than "death" or "occupation". Yes, "to croak", be eaten by worms, and have no one to care for me or the children. Who'll bring up those little bundles of flesh?'

A worker at a nearby table spoke up: 'And don't forget the upper class, my friends, with their five-storey apartment buildings.' He spoke with bitter resentment. 'When I asked one of them for a decent wage like everyone else, he told me I should be ashamed of myself. He had the nerve to say that by working for him at half wages I was performing a patriotic duty. I told him that life was getting more expensive all the time, but he just went on about patriotism! I told him that a hand in the fire's different from a hand in water but still he talked about patriotism. "Fine," I said. "How come I'm the only one with a patriotic duty?" He replies, "Other people should perform theirs too." "Oh yes? And what about you?", I say. "You shouldn't speak to me like that", he answers. "I don't need someone like you to remind me of my duty. And, after all, you can easily see how bad my economic situation is."

'So I tell him: "All I can see is your five-storey building!" "God save me from the envious," he quotes in reply. "Beware of evil from those you've been good to." I flung his miserable wage packet right in his face and yelled, "Here, take it! I'm going 'over there' tomorrow!" He said, "They've really turned you into a money-grubber, haven't they? You've lost all sense of honour!" That made me mad as hell, and I told him "Not one of us went over to them before you did. Weren't you the very first to put your hand in theirs? What do you call that agency your company has? A 'patriotic duty'?"'

The stink of cheap tobacco filled Usama's nostrils. His head throbbed in response to the conversation, so full of hatred.

'Five, six! A perfect score, Abu Nawwaf!' shouted a man playing backgammon. 'A terrific score, bigger than your moustache! Ha! Ha! Ha! Order yourself some tea; it's on me!'

Usama stared in amazement at the man's laughing face. It was Shahada! Impossible! What had he done to himself? What had Israel's 'civilization' done to him?

Shahada wore a leather jacket with a fur collar. His curly hair stood out around his head like a giant halo in an Afro at least four inches high. Thick sideburns sprouted like miniature hedges on both sides of his face. In his hand, adorned with an expensive gold ring, he held a pipe, and he spoke out of the corner of his mouth, like some big foreign film star.

So that's how you ended up, Shahada! By Jesus, killing you would be no crime, by Moses and Muhammad too! And where's Adil, who's sunk so low himself? Oh, Adil! How you break my heart, my old friend.

Adil had come in with Zuhdi, and was greeted from all sides. Shahada did not speak, however, but went on drawing on his pipe, with the superior expression demanded by his high status as a successful businessman.

Adil spoke gently, standing directly over the other man: 'Shahada, how are you? How come you don't say hello to me? Strangers speak to me, but not you; how come?'

Shahada waved his hand with its gold ring and spoke out of the corner of his mouth. 'Hello; how are you?' he muttered, his pipe still clenched in his teeth. Then he clapped his hands imperiously and shouted, 'Waiter! Bring some coffee for our friends!'

'No thank you,' said Adil. He smiled. 'Please don't put yourself out, Shahada.'

'Why not? Aren't we good enough for you?' Shahada's words were a challenge. He stared at Adil's working clothes as he said this, then turned up the fur collar of his jacket and tapped his large gold ring on the table. 'Hey, Muhammad! Bring coffee for the lads. Yes, for everyone, for everyone here.'

The café owner spoke from behind his counter: 'You're going to pay for everyone?'

'Everyone, yourself included,' Shahada responded defiantly. 'Come on, Muhammad, here you are.'

He produced a wallet stuffed with banknotes and took out a single large blue note. He handed it ostentatiously to Muhammad, all the while peering at Adil from beneath his heavy eyelids. 'Are you watching, Adil?' he seemed to be saying.

Adil sat down opposite Shahada: 'There's no need for that, my friend. Why put yourself out?'

Shahada's expression was like that of a fighting cock ready for battle: 'Don't worry, there's plenty more where that came from, thanks be to God. Shall I get you a water-pipe?'

Adil laughed loudly and made a simple gesture of acceptance. 'Well, since you've got plenty of money and insist on throwing it around, I've no objection.'

Shahada relaxed and looked pleased. 'Bring a water-pipe too, Muhammad,' he shouted. 'What about you, Zuhdi, you want one too?'

'No,' said Zuhdi diffidently, 'I'll share Adil's.'

Shahada gave him a contemptuous look. 'Come on, Zuhdi, that's not right,' he said. 'I can handle that and a lot more besides. Another water-pipe, Muhammad.'

He looked at the pipe in his hand. 'If I weren't so used to this,' he said, 'I'd order a water-pipe for myself, but I don't like to change what I'm smoking. And cigarettes cause awful problems, they say. Yes, I saw a film on TV – my own TV, in fact – about lung cancer and its relationship to smoking. Then I asked one of my doctor friends and he told me pipe smoking's the least harmful.'

Usama watched Shahada's exaggerated gestures and burned with rage. Have you forgotten the cheap cigarettes of your past?, he thought. Why don't you give some of this great advice to your father, my fine fellow? God help your poor father! Go on, enjoy yourself, my friend, strut around and be happy. Let Israel strut like a turkey-cock and do what it wants with us. And you, Adil, sink right down, and enjoy a nice water-pipe at the expense of this shit Shahada! Who was it used to piss in the trough? Come on, Shahada! Why don't you have a nice piss now? Piss on your Arab heritage, piss on your nation and your homeland, go ahead, you can do it as long as the likes of Adil let you pay for their water-pipes.

'How's your father, Shahada?' Adil asked gently. 'Well, I trust?'

Shahada peered closely at him, to see whether the question was intended to be sarcastic. But Adil's expression seemed genuine, devoid of malice.

'He's fine, thanks be to God,' Shahada answered shortly.

Then he remembered to return the inquiry. 'How about yourself, how's your father?'

Adil's voice was strained. 'Bad to worse. His condition goes on deteriorating, poor man.'

Shahada said, with enviable smoothness, 'If only we're lucky enough to live so long! Ah, yes, we each have our allotted span.'

The man's voice was full of malice, and Usama thought his head would burst in fury. Suddenly he stood up and stormed over to Adil, interrupting the conversation: 'Adil! A word with you.'

Adil stared at him in amazement and Zuhdi's eyes nearly popped out of his head. 'Why don't you say hello to everyone, Usama?' Adil said quietly.

For the first time Usama's eyes now met those of Shahada, who burst out in childlike delight and surprise: 'Usama!'

Usama smiled coldly. 'You still remember me?' he asked sarcastically.

The childlike expression vanished from Shahada's face, and was replaced by an angry glower. He puffed hard on his pipe.

Adil spoke: 'Shahada, Abu Ahmad that is, has invited us to have coffee. Why don't you join us?'

Impatiently, Usama shook his head. 'No, I need you now, this minute. It's very important.'

'Come on,' Adil said lightly. 'I'm not leaving now and missing the water-pipe Abu Ahmad's offering me.'

Adil's compliment had its desired magical effect. Though he still seemed somewhat apprehensive in the face of Usama's attitude, Shahada now said with pride, if not complete confidence, 'Come, you must let me buy you a coffee. I've ordered it for everybody, it's on me. If you like, I'll order a water-pipe for you too.'

Usama neither answered nor looked at him.

'Didn't you hear me, sir?' Shahada demanded angrily. 'I said you're to drink a coffee, on me.'

'No thanks,' Usama replied. 'I don't want any.'

Shahada opened his eyes wide. A vein swelled on his forehead. 'My coffee isn't good enough for you?' he asked. 'Your cousin here's going to drink my coffee, and smoke my water-pipe too. Why won't you?'

Usama understood the insult and broke out in a cold sweat. He was furious with Shahada. This is just too much, Adil! he thought. You let this cheap bastard talk about you that way and just sit there like an idiot! By God, murdering such people would be no crime.

He invented a lie. 'My mother's very ill,' he said. 'She might even die tonight. Please come.'

Adil rose, followed by Zuhdi. 'Anything you want, Usama,' he said anxiously.

Shahada relaxed and the rage left his eyes.

Adil headed towards the Saada neighbourhood, but Usama caught him by the arm.

'Please come this way,' he said.

Adil's eyes expressed his surprise.

'Please come. I want us to understand each other,' said Usama.

Adil realized what he wanted. He followed his cousin down the alley he'd chosen. Darkness had fallen over the town. The streets were empty. People stayed at home after dark, for fear of the surprises that night might bring.

'Why are you avoiding me?' asked Usama reproachfully. 'For days I've been trying to meet you alone to continue the conversation we started the other evening. But you avoid me as if I were a military patrol.'

His cousin walked on in silence.

'Adil, I don't know how to begin, but you know that the way you're acting is wrong. What would people say about us, Adil? Don't you see you're setting a bad example to the other men? And what if your father found out that you're working over there, in Israel, like a common labourer? Have you thought of that? I tell you, he'd prefer to die a thousand deaths rather than see his son sink as low as this.'

Thoughts crowded into his mind. Fragments of memory, of what Adil had said about his father: 'He hangs onto life as the past does to the present, as a prison record clings to an ex-convict, as a virus to a living cell. And I'm that cell.

Every element in my own body has become a slave to his illnesses.'

'Why are you smiling, Adil? Explain. Say something, anything. You weren't born to do this kind of work. Not just because you're furthering the enemy's interests, but because you're qualified for better things. Speak, Adil, say something. Defend yourself. Tell me honestly, are you content with what you're doing?'

'Content?' Adil burst out. 'Contentment! That's a commodity nobody can buy on the West Bank any more, or in Gaza. Contentment indeed! What the hell are you talking about?'

'Adil, don't let pride carry you away. There's no shame in taking advice from someone younger than yourself, but to persist in doing wrong is truly shameful.'

Adil didn't reply. Usama was suddenly enraged. 'Why don't you say something?' he cried. 'Defend yourself, for God's sake! Are you happy with the way things are? Does it please you to sink down to the level of Zuhdi, Shahada and Abu Nawwaf? They're ignorant, they don't know what they're doing. But you! You're in agony, I can tell. Everything you told me that evening makes me certain that you're suffering. And that makes me sad; it makes me miserable. Ever since I arrived here, everything's been bringing me closer to the brink of madness. They've made you greedy, Adil, they've broken your spirit. And I don't see the faintest glimmer of shame in your eyes. That's just too much. I don't understand.'

Usama paused, but Adil still didn't speak. He began again. 'And to see you in the café with Shahada! Shahada, who's betrayed you, you with whom he's shared bread and salt over the years; Shahada, who's abandoned the country and everything in it for the sake of a gold ring, a fancy pipe and a wallet stuffed with money. But what's worst of all is that you just smile at his insults, as if he were an equal or a friend. Didn't you see him staring at your clothes? Didn't you hear the way he bragged, with that loud mouth of his?

He's forgotten the cheap tobacco he used to smoke, thinks he's come up in the world with that fancy pipe of his!'

Adil finally spoke. 'So what if Shahada smokes a pipe?' he asked wearily. 'Does that somehow diminish your dignity or mine? Shahada's free to do whatever he wants – and that includes smoking a pipe.'

'But that business about the television!' Usama broke in angrily. 'Didn't you hear him say: "my own TV", in that tone of voice?'

'Can't you see? Shahada's trying to move up into the ranks of our own illustrious class, and we're still far ahead of him in such matters.'

'What about those gloating remarks about your father's illness? He was actually insolent!'

'That's perfectly natural,' said Adil. 'Shahada never liked my father. Now's his chance to get back at him.'

'But Adil, he's taking revenge on you too.'

'Well, you know the proverb. "When fathers eat sour grapes, it's their children's teeth that ache."'

Usama's anger welled up. 'Why do you talk that way?' he cried. 'Try to understand *me*, for God's sake! You're driving me crazy! All this because Shahada ordered you a cup of coffee and a water-pipe?'

Adil merely smiled disdainfully.

'I'm sorry,' Usama said quickly. 'I didn't mean to insult you. But I can't understand your attitude. Why do you defend that guy? Don't you think he deserves a punch in the mouth?'

'No.'

'Adil.' Usama was pleading now. 'Do you want us to reach an understanding or not?'

'We'll never understand each other.'

'Why? Because you've become like them?'

'No, Usama, I haven't become *like* them. I'm *one* of them. I think that makes you more ashamed than angry.'

Usama shook his head sadly. Rothschild indeed! And the poem about the sacrificial lamb. Sink into the mud, my country! Sink!

He burst out uncontrollably, 'I don't believe it. I'll never believe it. I just don't believe you've forgotten your own country and the occupation!'

'The proof that I haven't forgotten my country is that I haven't left it.'

Usama felt the knife twist in his heart. 'I only left for a short time,' he said. 'And I've come back, as you see. If I'd forgotten it, I wouldn't have come back.'

Adil smiled and dropped another bombshell: 'But your mother told me they fired you. Isn't that true?'

Usama stopped in the road and beat his chest with his fist: 'Are you implying that if they hadn't fired me, I wouldn't have returned? Is that it? Speak up, Adil. Is that what you mean?'

'You can take it any way you like.'

'The only way I can take it is that you, like everyone else here, have abandoned the revolutionary movement. Our people abroad have noticed this, and they write about it all the time now.'

'Write about it, do they? Let them live the way we live here, then we'd see what sort of problems came up.'

'I don't mean other people. I mean *our own* people.'

'Who are you talking about? The Palestinians in Kuwait, Dhahran and the Gulf? Let them help build industries in the West Bank and Gaza and we'd stop working "inside" straight away. But they won't do that. You know why? Because they don't want to risk their money; yet they want *us* to bear all the burdens of risk and sacrifice on our own.'

'Yes,' Usama agreed. 'And that's exactly what we have to do. It's we who are responsible for resistance, us first and last.'

'And if we starve, how can we resist?'

'Hunger will make revolution explode.' Usama stopped. 'Why are you smiling? It's a well-known theory. Don't you understand?'

'And these "people" you talk about, do they go hungry?

Look, friend, those people pile up their cash, and buy stocks and bonds and real estate in Beirut and Europe. What about you, how come you left right after the occupation began?'

'I just couldn't stand it. I couldn't bear to watch them walking our streets, violating the sanctity of our country.'

'Great! Superb! Magnificent! That's the essence of resistance, all right.'

'You speak in the same bitter tone as Zuhdi, Shahada and the bread seller,' said Usama. 'All you have to do now is taunt me for wearing trousers and a shirt that have been ironed!'

Adil stared hard at him but didn't reply. Then he hurried on ahead towards a bar. Usama caught up with him and took him by the arm: 'Come on, I haven't finished yet. Don't run away from me. We must reach an understanding.'

'My throat's dry,' Adil replied coldly.

He went into the bar while Usama stood outside cursing. What a gutless nation! God almighty! God of the chosen race! Devils of the accursed race! Drink up, Adil, drink up! I'm waiting here in the doorway mourning for our nation, for the 'disaster' of '48, and for the 'set-back' of '67 still glowering at me from beyond the bridge over the Jordan. Mourning while the hopes of a lifetime are spilled at the doors of taverns.

Adil emerged swaying from the bar. 'Here, Usama,' he said. 'Take a swig of this. There's a genie in this bottle. Drink up and forget. Forget your troubles, my tired friend. Drink! Drink to my father's health. Drink to the kidney machine and to the catheter.'

Adil raised the bottle. 'Our people are being killed by the dozen; Abu Sabir's fingers are cut off by the blade of his saw. Come on, drink up and forget. This damned life has no mercy. It plucks the hair from your body. It stands your hair on end. Drink up. Here's to the kidney machine and the catheters!'

'Adil, there are orders to blow up the buses.'

And who's going to blow them up, Adil thought? You, Usama? Is it you? What about that elegy for the sacrificial lamb, who composed that? It was you. But that was just ink on paper. Oh, you pillars of justice in the great Arab capitals! Oh, what judgements, what condemnations! Shahada's the accused standing in the dock. And the charge is smoking a pipe!

They mounted the steps of the Fatimia College. There were workers standing on ladders and hanging long coloured streamers between the buildings. The paper decorations fluttered and rustled in the breeze, making a sound almost like moaning.

'Tomorrow's the feast day,' Adil murmured. 'The celebrations for the birth of the Prophet. Paper streamers and lights! The upper classes expiate their sins. Rejoice, oh Muhammad!'

He stopped in front of the college and stood motionless.

'Yes,' he said, 'they were standing here, long lines of them, hunger suppressing their cries. They weren't weeping, but I could see the grief and fury in their eyes. Women, children, old men – and men like you and me, Usama.'

He staggered as he turned round, and shouted, 'And who are all these decorations for? Who's going to enjoy them? Decorations, my foot! They're garlands cast upon the graves of our victims. Will those palm fronds bring the dead back to life? And you ask me whether I'm content!' Adil's voice was heavy with sarcasm. 'You composer of a precious elegy long ago for a single lamb! Let me tell you, my friend, lambs are still being brought to the sacrifice, and who cares? Yes, let those pillars of the community do their judging in the Arab capitals! The tragedy's much greater than Shahada's pipe and the Egged buses. What about the money given for the resistance? What's happened to it, who's going to account for it? And the blue bread and the loaves made with dust sweepings. Have you heard about the blue bread?'

Suddenly, from the mountains above the city, shots rang out. Usama listened and then whispered anxiously, 'Listen, Adil. The comrades are active. Listen. Just listen!'

Searchlights were switched on and one of the houses was flooded with light. They could hear the sound of army vehicles moving towards the mountains, the tanks beginning their slow, grinding climb. The men stringing paper streamers climbed down the ladders and quickly disappeared into the neighbouring houses. Usama watched what was going on and said to himself, 'What am I doing? The resistance units are active and I stand here listening to the ramblings of a drunk!'

The sound of battle increased. Tanks came to a halt in front of the house under suspicion and began to fire. Hand grenades and shells exploded. The blare of sirens sounded from the army vehicles; the firing of rockets and the clatter of machine-guns were all around them.

'Come on. There'll be a curfew. They might suspect us, Adil.'

'You know about the blue bread?'

'No, and I don't want to. Come on Adil, let's go.'

'Who's responsible for the blue bread and Shahada's pipe?'

'How can you ramble on about blue bread and Shahada's pipe when our comrades are fighting? Come on, let's get out of here. The town's closing down. They'll declare a curfew in a minute. Just look at that house – it's like a scene from hell!'

'But tomorrow, dear friend, everyone will be making ululating sounds of joy. Have you ever heard of a nation that welcomes disaster with cries of joy?'

'Yes, I have. And I wish you'd do the same.'

'Here, have a swig. There's a genie in this bottle. Drink up and forget. Forget your troubles, my tired friend.'

'That bottle of yours is a curse. Our comrades are using Molotov cocktails while you stick to your bottle. Give it here! I'll break it over the head of each member of the Karmi family!'

'Why don't you? Then tomorrow we'll hear the cries of joy ring out. Have you ever heard of a people that welcomes disaster with cries of joy?'

'Yes, I have. I swear I have.'

Um Sabir was shouting, 'Hey, Itaf! Ask Um Badawi if she's got any spare flour.'

As the child made her way across the roof, an Israeli soldier shouted, 'Get down! Get down! You can't go up there.'

Um Sabir beat her breast in distress. 'What a wretched life! How can I feed my children? It's enough to break your heart, this life! What'll we do if the curfew goes on for another two days?'

All over the old part of town, the women gathered at their windows trying to borrow whatever they could from each other. The situation was desperate. Most of those who lived in the old neighbourhood were labourers, green-grocers, butchers, or sellers of *falafil* and *tamriyya*;* they were generally poor and kept nothing in store. The children were cooped up inside the small houses, driving their mothers mad. One child was under a bed, another on top of a cupboard, a baby was screaming, husbands were venting their anger on their innocent wives.

Abu Sabir murmured, 'Forgive us, oh Lord, deliver us!' Zuhdi cursed the day he'd been spared the sandstorms of Kuwait. 'I'll go crazy if I ever taste lentils again,' he said, and threw his slipper at one of the children; this brought a

---

* *Falafil*: savoury cakes made of vegetables and fried in oil. *Tamriyya*: a sweet pastry sold at certain hours of the day by street peddlers.

chorus of wails from all sides. 'God curse whoever fathered you, you curs!' he shouted. His wife Saadiyya suddenly opened the door, letting the children run free. 'Out!' she yelled. 'Get out! Go and pester the Jews instead of getting on my nerves!' Um Sabir did the same and her husband exploded: 'You're crazy, woman! The streets are full of Jewish soldiers!'

But children were now emerging from all the houses, at first lurking in dark corners like mice, staring out at the soldiers and laughing and winking at one another. The soldiers wore helmets and carried machine-guns. A little boy ran from one house to the next, and a soldier yelled and swore at him. The children's laughter echoed down the street as they imitated the soldier's oaths. Another boy tied a tomato can to a cat's tail and sent the animal running. A soldier swung and pointed his gun at the boy. But the children, delighted at the game, laughed even louder. The soldiers began to chase the boys, who scampered home, slamming the doors behind them. Then out they came again. A soldier caught one of them and started to beat him, and the mothers let loose a stream of curses on all who'd had a hand in the creation of the state. Their husbands blinked in surprise at the volley of oaths.

A tank passed, all four sides bristling with guns; the weight of its metal tracks crushed the old paving stones. The children shrank deeper into the shadowy corners of the houses till the tank had gone, then ran out after it, chanting: 'Fatah! . . . PLO . . . Fatah! . . . PLO . . .' The soldiers shouted curses and aimed their weapons at the children, sending them dashing for cover again. But a little boy of six stood his ground, unzipped his faded trousers and pointed his penis at the soldiers, as though affirming the principle of self-defence. The street exploded in an uproar of shouts as the boys seemed suddenly filled with insane bravado. A soldier seized two of them by the scruffs of the neck and dangled them like a pair of plucked pigeons. After thrashing them soundly, he pushed them both into a patrol car.

The girls began to beat out a rhythm on empty margarine cans. And the boys went on screaming out the PLO slogan: 'Revolution! Revolution until victory! Revolution! Revolution until victory!'

Um Sabir leaned half-way out of the window and yelled at the soldier who was mistreating the children: 'May God break your arm! May seventy evil eyes get you! May your children all die young! May God destroy you, by the glory of the Prophet Muhammad!'

The children's chanting and clapping rang through the empty streets, a crescendo of rhyming slogans about God, Palestine, Arab unity, the Popular Front, the Democratic Front, freedom, dedication, self-sacrifice and Yasser Arafat.

But throughout the din, engineers of the so-called Israeli Defence Forces went on measuring the height and width of an old house at the end of the street. People ran out of the doomed house, the men with beds and mattresses on their backs, the women carrying their belongings to their neighbours' houses. And then everything went quiet. People hid in the corners of their homes, their windows open but their ears tightly shut. Then came the explosion.

The walls of the old house crumbled. In one massive piece, the roof caved in and settled on the rubble. Clouds of smoke rose from the ruins. The old man whose house it had been stood on a neighbouring roof and called out the *adhan*,* his voice breaking: '*Allahu Akbar!* God is most great!'

'God is most great!' repeated the neighbours in unison. Gathered at the windows, the women raised their voices in loud ululations, while the girls continued to beat out a rhythm on the empty tin cans. A single piercing girlish voice began the song of solidarity once again. The boys took up the melody until the whole street was filled with the cry, 'Palestine! Palestine!'

* *Adhan*: the Muslim call to prayer, sounded from the minarets five times a day.

Usama, watching from a window, found he had tears in his eyes. So all was well, in fact. He saw Basil standing in a corner alternately chanting: 'We're all the men of Yasser Arafat' and 'Revolution! Revolution until victory!'

Two soldiers grabbed Basil, who offered little resistance. They covered his head with a sackcloth hood and shoved him into a patrol car, while his sister Nuwar stared dumbfounded from a window. 'Whatever God wills, so be it,' his father could be heard shouting. 'But what came over the boy? Does he think he can free Palestine all by himself?' The boy's mother burst into tears. Nuwar looked coldly at her father's frozen face, then turned back to the window as though to reassure herself that the children had not been cowed, but were still energetically beating their drums and chanting:

Kalashnikovs will destroy the tanks!
RPGs* will bring down the warplanes!

* RPG: the initials of the Russian name for a Soviet rocket launcher.

At dawn the patrol cars began touring the city, the loud-speakers announcing the end of the curfew. People seemed to heave a collective sigh of relief. The old men of the Saada neighbourhood streamed towards the great mosque to say their prayers. The greengrocers reopened their shops and began to clear out their rotting produce, tossing it into the streets, filling the rubbish bins with the remains of decaying, stinking fish. Children came out to buy flour, tea and sugar for their mothers. And the workers, their eyes still heavy with sleep, made their way once more towards the Egged buses and back to work.

'Morning, mate.'

'Morning to you.'

'The bastards have taken Hamada in,' reported Zuhdi, walking along at Adil's side.

'Basil too,' was Adil's gloomy reply.

'The sandstorms of Kuwait were more merciful than this.' He glanced at Adil's scowling face, then let out a dry laugh: 'It'll all work out in the end,' he said.

Adil thought about that for a moment. All work out, would it? When? The houses blown up, the killings, the imprisonments, Usama's ideas, Nuwar's enigmatic smile, the gurgling sound of the kidney machine while Basil slept on a mat in some prison. And his valiant father didn't even bother to ask where his own son was, although he'd certainly turn the event into a dramatic and heroic incident when he talked to the television reporters. He'd raise his head high and announce to his neighbours: 'Yes, that's my son; that's my son all right!'

'Prison's for men.' Zuhdi forced a laugh.

'No,' said Adil. 'It's for the youngsters, the boys. While the men go off in Egged buses to complete the construction of the state.'

They walked in silence. 'Well, even that's better than emigration, isn't it?' demanded Zuhdi, defending himself and the rest. He jerked his head in Adil's direction, appealing for a response. His companion nodded, as he'd done a thousand times before: 'Yes, of course.'

'And there are many grown men in prison. Women too.'

'Yes,' agreed Adil.

Salih, Elias, Hamza, Antun, Naila, Yusra, Amal, Fatihiyya and Maryam. While I'm here, thought Adil. On my own. Wandering the streets of Tel Aviv, repeating words that have no meaning and get no response. 'Shared oppression.' 'The greed of the Israeli bourgeoisie.' 'Exploitation by international capitalism.' But Shlomo's a victim too, he thought. Then there was 'freedom', 'brotherhood', 'equality', 'justice', 'peace'. All lost in a bottomless abyss. I'm talking to myself. Those who would listen are behind prison walls, while I'm here alone, wandering the streets of Tel Aviv. God damn this life! But I'm not really alone. I'm with them, with Zuhdi and the others. And my role's no meaner than any other. Even if idiots don't understand.

He looked up. Towards the east, the sky was deep blue. The rays of the spring sun were boring through distant clouds, and the buds and blooms absorbed the light greedily. The pines on the heights of Mount Aibal swam in a space of eternal hope. A cool breeze rustled the leaves of the trees in front of the town hall; they glistened and shone. Spring. Hope. Dreams of freedom and peace.

He was suddenly overcome with a feeling of love, which overwhelmed all sense of weakness and defeat. He declared optimistically, 'Abu Sabir must receive due compensation. We must adopt a new approach. Step by step we must learn how to become masters and not victims.'

Zuhdi agreed enthusiastically: 'Exactly! Right on, man. You say the word and we'll do what we have to do.'

Adil teased him, 'But what about the sandstorms of Kuwait?'

'Look, man! You believe everything I say? I swear – just to sit in the Humuz Café means the world to me.'

They climbed onto the bus with everyone else and took seats at the back; each was thinking of the substantial security deposit he'd have to make. They were frowning by the time they reached the factory, where Adil made for the garage and the rest dispersed around the site.

The Israeli workers had assembled in front of the machine shop, listening grimly to the foreman, who stood before them speaking in Hebrew and gesturing expansively.

'Zuhdi, come over here,' an inspector called.

What do they want now? wondered Zuhdi. Wasn't Hamada enough? If one of them so much as uses the word *Aravim* to me, I'll split his head open with this wrench, he thought.

He remembered what Adil had said. Was it true that these men were exploited just as he was, equally deceived and misled? Were they too victims of economic interests, used to satisfy the ambitions of a select few? But in time of war they put on their helmets, take up their machine-guns and shoot to kill. And who was it then who'd taken Hamada? And Basil, Salih and the other young men and women who sat in prison. He shook his head, confused by his thoughts, and gripped his wrench. If one of them calls me *Aravim* I'll let him have it all right, even if it's the angel Gabriel himself!

'Tell them yourself, Zuhdi,' said the inspector. 'Isn't the price of sugar in Amman the same as in Israel?'

'Yes, exactly the same,' replied Zuhdi, with a cunning, gloating expression. 'In Amman a pound of sugar costs no more than 4 qurush.'

The workers began shouting and shaking their fists. Zuhdi went on proudly, 'And in Syria a pound of sugar costs only 3 qurush, and a loaf of bread costing only half a qirsh will feed an entire family.'

The men opened their eyes in amazement and their gestures became more dramatic, their arguing louder.

'You're quite sure of what you're saying?' demanded the inspector angrily.

'Absolutely sure,' smiled Zuhdi, and walked away, leaving the group still locked in a storm of angry argument. Gesturing with his wrench, Zuhdi grinned maliciously. Who'd pay for Hamada's fear, for Saadiyya's tears and those of the thousands like her living in misery and sorrow? He looked back at the Israeli workers. They'd stopped arguing now and looked tired and strained. Zuhdi felt sorry for them; he was confused. Maybe they were oppressed after all, like everyone else. If they were living a life of luxury they certainly wouldn't have cared so much about the price of sugar and bread. They are privileged, though, he reminded himself. The lowest-paid of them make twice as much as any Arab worker, no matter how skilled or experienced. They enjoy privileges that Adil himself has never achieved. They eat their lunch in clean rooms, sitting on chairs at tables. They're paid extra for travel and given cost-of-living increments, and they're eligible for social security, old-age pensions and disability payments. They elect members to the Knesset. But we have no Knesset, no army, no government. How can Adil say that Shlomo has more in common with me than the owner of the olive-oil factory at Jift! Impossible! I don't believe it.

It was perhaps an hour later that Shlomo came over and asked, 'Did you hear the news broadcast?'

Zuhdi shook his head and bent over the engine he was working on.

Shlomo's voice expressed his hatred: 'Terrorists with Katyushas have attacked Bisan; they burned a house and killed a civilian and a woman.'

Zuhdi went on working and didn't reply.

Shlomo pushed ahead, provocatively: 'You don't have anything to say. Does that mean you admire their actions?'

Zuhdi smiled and asked coolly, 'What're you talking about?'

'Didn't you hear what I said?'

'Did you say something?'

'I was telling you about a terrorist attack in Bisan.'

'What did they do?'

'Didn't you hear?'

'No.'

'They killed a civilian and a woman and burned a house down.'

Oh, great! Adil says the fighting will end one day and people will live like brothers. They'll all wear the same clothes, eat the same food, take milk from the same nipple. What rubbish! I don't believe a word of it. You can't believe everything you hear. Damn the Arab leaders and Israel! They've taught us to doubt everything.

'And what else? Did they do anything else?'

'They kill a woman and a civilian and burn down a house, and you want them to do something else?'

Killed a woman, did they? How many women have you killed, you, poor, oppressed Shlomo, who'll live with me like a brother one fine imaginary day? And they killed a civilian too? Don't you remember the massacres of Arab civilians at Bahr al-Baqr, Deir Yassin, and Qibya?* And they burned down a house? How many houses have you bastards blown up? Just yesterday, Shlomo, you blew one up in the Saada district. Yes, thanks to the engineers of the 'Defence Forces'. Before you there were the British, before them the Turks, and so on back into time immemorial.

Shlomo gave him a rough, friendly slap on the shoulder.

* The reference is to three Palestinian villages in which massacres of civilians were committed in 1947, 1948, and 1953 respectively.

The wrench slipped out of Zuhdi's hand and he lost his balance, falling over the engine. In trying to break his fall he cut his hand on a sharp piece of metal and his palm began to bleed.

'What's wrong with you?' Shlomo laughed. 'I'm talking to you, man, and you're not taking any notice.'

Zuhdi pulled himself up, gripping his big wrench and trying to calm down. He hoped the man would leave before he lost control of himself. Go away, Shlomo. God protect you! I know it wasn't you that blew up the house in Saada, that you're not responsible for putting Hamada and Basil and the rest in prison. But yet in some way you're to blame too, you're responsible but not responsible!

Shlomo began to walk away, muttering, 'Terrorists! *Aravim mouloukhlakhim!*'*

Zuhdi spun round and shouted, 'What did you say, Shlomo?'

Shlomo turned, his face showing surprise and apprehension. He stared at the raised wrench in Zuhdi's hand.

'What did you say, Shlomo? Say it again! I dare you!'

'I wasn't talking about you,' replied Shlomo, stepping back.

'What did you say?'

'Nothing.'

'You did.'

'No, nothing.'

'Yes, you did.'

'I didn't.'

'You said *Aravim mouloukhlakhim.*'

'Okay, so I did.'

'I've got something to say, too. Take this . . .'

Shlomo let out a yell and men came running to his aid. Abu Nawwaf put down his tools and called the Arab workers. In a moment the two groups were locked in a

---

Mouloukhlakhim: 'dirty' in Hebrew. The expression 'dirty Arabs' is a common racist epithet.

vicious battle, though no one thought to ask the reason for the quarrel.

Abu Nawwaf fell to the ground screaming. Adil tried to separate the men, to solve the Middle East conflict all by himself, but all he got was a heavy blow to the head, and his conciliatory words were drowned in a sea of violent curses. His right ear took another blow, so sharp that the earth seemed to spin. Flailing wrenches, pliers and planks of wood flew through the air. Adil took another sharp blow on his right cheek and yelled angrily, 'I'm not Christ, for God's sake!'

'Shared injustice' was forgotten now, along with 'promises of peace', 'dreams of brotherhood' and 'workers' rights'. Adil fought like a madman, the battle now more meaningful to him than any fine words of peace. In the end, he thought, only the hammer protects what's inside the head.

The ground was soon littered with injured men and the ambulances began to arrive, their sirens screaming. The inspector and other officials appeared and the wounded were taken to hospital. Zuhdi was arrested by the police. The other Arab workers climbed into the bus, leaving the factory and their day's wages behind them.

Basil had trouble opening his eyes. There were many faces staring down at him. He raised a hand to ward off a slap in the face, and the movement sent pain through his body mercilessly like an electric current. He shut his eyes tight, and the tears came as he thought of his mother and of Adil . . . They'll beat me again, he thought. I spat in their faces and shouted, 'Revolution! Revolution until victory!' Oh, victory demands a high price! He gritted his teeth and groaned.

A hand gently rubbed his aching shoulder. Opening his eyes and staring up into the sea of faces, he settled on one he knew well. 'Salih!' he shouted eagerly.

Then he fainted again. He was gently stroked and fed tea from a spoon, and his face was wiped with a wet cloth. Someone shouted encouragingly, 'Congratulations! You can take it! And more! Come on, up you go, Basil, you're a man now!'

Gradually life seeped back into his body, and hope and pride surged within him. So I've become a man. No teacher will ever dare to call me 'boy' again.

Sitting up on the mat he told them the latest news from the outside world, and they listened eagerly. The Habash house had been demolished and the Hawash house shelled. It was said that Abu Ammar, Yasser Arafat himself, had been with the guerrillas. Many Israeli soldiers had been killed and the patrol cars had carried away dozens of injured. The guerrillas had escaped to the East Bank; some had been killed and others captured. As for Basil, they'd put a sack over his head and taken him to their headquarters, but he'd spat in their faces and they'd beaten him badly.

'May you live to get the same again, Basil! Prison's for men, you know.' 'We'll have a party for you such as the world's never seen.' 'Hold your head up high and never let it fall. Prison's for men, Abu al-Izz!'

Abu al-Izz, eh? Is that who I am, 'father of glory'? That's really great! I've become one of them for sure. How fantastic to be the 'father' of something, something to look after, to protect, to take pride in. Abu al-Izz! A great name. The finest thing that's ever been said or ever could be said.

The conversation went on for a long time. He got to know all his comrades, who treated him with great respect and called him Abu al-Izz. The title filled him with pride. A superb name, the finest name of all!

Salih asked eagerly, 'What about Adil? And your father, and Nuwar? Have you seen my family? How are my mother and Lina?'

'Adil's fine. Father goes from bad to worse. Nuwar's in a bad way – she's always crying.'

He stared apprehensively at Salih, and then whispered, 'You love her, don't you?'

Salih looked down and didn't answer.

'Your sister Lina visits us all the time,' Basil went on. 'But I haven't seen your mother for ages. If I'd known I was coming here, I'd have visited her! But I didn't plan on this.'

'Maybe you should plan on something like this in the future. You won't be here long. The sentence for spitting isn't that heavy. A few days. Maybe weeks. Then you'll leave. Will you be back?'

Embarrassed by the question, Basil stared in bewilderment at the faces of the 'brothers' around him. They began to laugh. Salih called, jokingly, 'Hey, Elias, come and meet Abu al-Izz.'

Elias left his corner and came over to them. Basil gasped when he saw the face and split lip. Yet the young man's one eye seemed to shine with happiness at the sight of the young 'guest' who'd divert the group for a few days and revive memories of home, family and sunshine.

Salih squeezed the young man's arm.

'Now Elias here,' he told Basil, 'is the best man among us. Just look at the badges of honour he wears on his face and hand.'

Elias held out his left hand in greeting: 'My *nom de guerre* is Abu Ahmad,' he said.

Then he laughed, his torn lips revealing his smashed teeth, the mutilated muscles of his face puckering up. Basil was horrified at the sight, but managed to stretch out a hand that was cold with sweat. While he shook Elias's left hand he glanced at his right; it was encased in black leather. Yes, victory demands a high price. The name Abu al-Izz wasn't that glorious after all, he told himself. I'm not making any plans for guerrilla action, not ever.

Dinner arrived. The forty prisoners gathered at the plastic bags spread out on the floor. Basil stared at the meal in surprise. A watery soup with a few bits of sweet pepper, tomato and courgette floating in it. Five olives. Half a green pepper. A small radish and a cup of tea. The soup was nauseating, he thought, but the prisoners were spooning it up greedily. He couldn't help noticing that everyone else had a boiled egg, but he was too shy to ask where his was. He did his best to force down some bread. Salih noticed that the boy wasn't eating. 'What's the matter, Basil?'

One of the prisoners laughed and said jokingly, 'Oh, Um Adil, please bring us some nice fried eggs and cheese. And don't forget the hors d'oeuvres: crushed aubergine and hummus, and tahina salad, and stuffed aubergine.'

They all laughed.

'No, Um Adil, don't do that,' said another man. 'We're on a strict diet here, we don't want to get fat. How about a nice salad, with lettuce, tomato and lemon? Or if you happen to have a bit of meat with parsley, garlic and pepper, I wouldn't complain.'

'Shut up, Hamza, God damn you,' another prisoner yelled, laughing, 'let us eat without choking.'

Salih handed Basil an egg. 'They give us eggs in the morning,' he explained, 'and we hide them for dinner. That's because it's a long time between sunset and bedtime; if all we had was this miserable dinner, we'd have to get through the evening on an empty stomach. Please take my egg, Basil, you're my guest tonight.'

Someone else shouted, 'Hey, you're my guest, too!'

'And mine!'

Basil soon had a pile of eggs in front of him, each prisoner insisting that he be his guest. Shyly he refused, insisting that eggs made him sick. The men all took their eggs back and Basil watched, feeling sad as they disappeared. Oh Mother, I never realized that eggs were such wonderful things! How beautiful they are! What a perfect, inimitable shape God's given them. Their thin shell is like a layer of cream on the dewy skin of a lovely young woman. And when you peel off the cream and touch the smiling face beneath, you shiver with sensual delight! What can be more lovely than an egg! The finest dish in the world, by the Prophet!

'You're sure you don't want it?' Salih asked as he took back his egg.

Basil shook his head and hid his face in the cup of black tea. The men gathered in groups at the far end of the room and began preparing the evening's programme. Salih sat on his mat with his books and papers, lost in the principles of political economy.

Elias was telling Basil his story. 'I was standing on the pavement in the main square, with the bomb in my hand. The coach passed right in front of me, full of tourists, I wanted to teach them a lesson for touring the occupied territories. But I was afraid that if I didn't hit the target just right, the bomb might be deflected onto the street and injure some of the townspeople. So I ran after the bus while it was still moving and grabbed hold of the metal window-frame so I could drop the bomb right inside. What I didn't realize was that the window was shut. So the bomb struck the glass first and exploded in my hand. No, don't feel sorry for me. There were more dead than wounded. But I lost an eye, a hand and part of my face, and my lip was split. Why do you look so sad?'

Basil's Adam's apple rose and fell visibly, but he forced himself to say, 'I'm not sad. But . . . oh, I just don't know.'

The name Abu al-Izz wasn't so glorious after all. In fact, it was terrifying. I'll never come back here, he thought. I'll never get involved in any guerrilla action.

Then the 'party' began. Hamza stood up and declared, 'Men! Revolutionary fighters of this generation! You who bear the torch of freedom in iron fists, lighting the path of justice and peace everywhere. We present to you this evening a bright new flame from Jabal al-Nar, our Mountain of Fire! A man who spat in the face of the tyrants and shouted like thunder: "Revolution! Revolution until victory!"'

The men responded in one voice, so loud the walls of the room seemed to shake: 'Revolution! Revolution until victory!'

'This evening,' Hamza went on, 'I present to you a valiant hero, a liberator of the homeland, Basil al-Karmi – known to us as Abu al-Izz.'

'Abu al-Izz! Abu al-Izz!' they all shouted.

Basil now found himself standing next to Hamza, with all eyes upon him. Overcome with fright, he had no idea what to say. He looked over to Salih for help and saw a broad smile on his friend's tanned face. Drawing strength from the jokes and encouraging comments around him, he began to speak with an almost childlike shyness: 'Brothers. Please forgive me if I don't manage to express myself very clearly. This is the first time I've ever made a speech. I don't know what to say, so let me just repeat to you what I said to the invaders of our country: "Revolution! Revolution until victory!"'

'Revolution! Revolution until victory,' the men burst out in chorus. Basil sat down again between Salih and Elias, hiding his shyness and emotion behind the shoulders of the two bigger men.

Someone began to sing:

Manacles on my wrists. Manacles on my wrists.
When they imprisoned me, they put manacles on
my wrists.
Oh son, my son,
I've got manacles on my wrists.
My brother and I are in gaol,
Guns surround us.
In prison we eat
Boiled lentils, mashed fish,
Manacles on my wrists. Manacles on my wrists.

Then came a poem by Kamal Nasser:*

Strike, executioner, we're not afraid.
These dark brows
Beaded with sweat
Are burdened with chains
So the nation will live.
Strike then, and have no fear!

One of the prisoners struck up a beat, using an empty bucket for a drum. A few men danced, while others lined up for the traditional folk dance, the *dabke*. The room was filled with claps, whistles and shouted slogans. Jokes were told. A poetry competition was held. The noisy party came to an end with a group anthem that brought a stream of

---

* Kamal Nasser was a Palestinian poet and political activist assassinated in Beirut in 1972 by an Israeli hit squad.

tears to Basil's eyes. He felt transported to a world he'd never known, one where pain and hope were intertwined and the will to live triumphed over prison walls:

> No, we'll not die, but we'll
> Uproot death from our land.
> There, over there, far, far away
> The soldiers will bear me, my friends,
> Casting me into the evil gloom.
> They searched my room, brother,
> But they found only books
> And my little brothers, starved and weak.
> They woke them up with their kicks
> And lit up anger in their eyes.
> My mother gave a long groan
> And my brothers screamed around her.
> And our neighbours crowded around them,
> Each with a son in gaol.
> And still my father's face appears
> Before me, arming me with hope.

Elias stood up; he'd removed the leather sheath from his mutilated arm. He raised it high, as a soldier lifts his country's flag, while the rest chanted:

> Over there I see a worker on the road.
> I see the victorious leader of the revolution.
> He waves to me with a hand of steel.
> A hail of sparks flies from his other hand!

Basil hid his face in his hands and wept bitterly. Victory demanded a high price. He lay down on his mat to sleep and turned to look at Salih, who lay next to him, bathed in the room's bright fluorescent light.

'Salih,' he murmured, 'when I leave here, I promise I won't answer to anyone unless they call me Abu al-Izz.'

'Great! The name is perfect for you.'

120

Dreamily, the boy went on, 'Yes, it's a fantastic name. The best. The best thing that's ever been said about me.'

He fell asleep holding Salih's hand, and dreamed that he lay at his mother's breast.

The light of dawn never penetrated the prison walls. There was no sunset, no night or day. The cells were flooded with bright fluorescent lighting at all times. At regular intervals an officer would walk through the block, count the prisoners and shout, 'All present', and then move on to each cell block in turn until all the men were accounted for.

'Wake up! Speak the name of God. Sleep's over, Hamza, you lazy devil! This is a mat, my boy, not a marriage bed!'

Basil stared around him, bewildered and depressed. Where am I? How long am I going to be here? I like being with the comrades. But they're all much older than me. And by tomorrow they'll have forgotten all about me, and I'll die of loneliness and boredom. Salih over there doesn't even speak. He goes to sleep with his books and wakes up to them too, just like Adil. What on earth does he do with all those books? If I had his degrees, I swear I'd never open another book as long as I lived. What's the good of books after you've got your degrees? Haj Abdullah's always telling us to study, and Hani says okay. What a bunch of lies I'm going to tell you, Hani, when I get out of here. Get ready for the fattest lies in history. First, I hit a soldier and an officer, that's right, and then I ripped the whip out of the hand of the guard who beats us up and really gave it to him. With one superb blow I tore out one of the officers' eyes and made him look like Elias. I tore his lip as he cursed my father. The soldiers were hammering on the door, but I

kept on hitting the officer and the soldier. The soldier died
and the officer fell to the ground, and lay wallowing in his
own blood. How about that, Hani? It's not so hard to
avenge Elias, after all. Why, you ask, did they let me go
after all that? Just listen, Hani. Bail money works wonders.
And then there was the Red Cross, and the mayor. He
helped, too, for your information, Hani.

Everyone began to talk at once. How's Abu al-Izz?
Good morning, my friend. It's morning; the night's over.
Come on, get up. Good morning, my friend! Good
morning, dear listener, good morning to you. Tum-tarum,
lum-lalum. Tara-lara-la-lum. Ah love, ah beauty and hope.
The guard's face reminds me of prehistory, of Darwin's
theory of evolution. Do not feel sad, dear listener, turn your
gaze towards Salih. Fill your heart with light. Tum-tarum,
lum-lalum. Tara, lara, lara-lalum. You're an active fellow,
dear listener. God damn you, Hamza! Get off that filthy
rotten mat of yours! Dear listener, we apologize for this
brief technical hitch. Now, back to love, beauty and hope.
Laughter, play, seriousness, love. Tarum, tara, lara-lara.
Bou, bou, ba-rum.

Basil laughed till he cried. He ate breakfast greedily. And
he gobbled up his boiled egg, which brought smiles to
several faces. They teased him a bit. 'Eggs don't agree with
you, right?' they asked.

The 'people's school' was now in session and the
prisoners broke up into small groups. In this corner, there
was basic literacy. Over there, preparation for elementary
school exams. In the far corner, high-school courses. Salih
and Elias worked hard. Hamza joked constantly and
noisily, swearing at everyone in turn.

Lunch was disgusting, but Basil ate ravenously all the
same. There was no time to feel sorry for himself. Even
Salih doesn't address me as 'boy', he thought. He smiles
now and then; he doesn't make me feel special, or completely neglected either. That's fine. But when I get out of
here, I'll outdo all the other kids and make their exploits

sound like child's play.

After lunch the men marched off to the prison workshop, where Basil, now known as Abu al-Izz, was set to work folding scores of plastic bags. He accepted his wage, eight Umar cigarettes, without gratitude. Umar was a rotten cheap brand, even worse than the local brand. The others divided up his cigarettes and offered him a puff here, a puff there. 'Don't pick up this filthy habit,' they warned him, 'just hand over those goodies.'

He ate his evening meal without hesitation and even found he enjoyed the tea. And he shouted out 'Allah' appreciatively when Antun sang his sad folk songs, drawing them out like the blue skies above the pines of Mount Aibal:

> My homeland, part of heaven,
> Your name is like a prayer upon my lips.'

The evening assembly began. Salih prepared his notes, wiped away his usual brief smile and spoke at length. Basil alias Abu al-Izz heard phrases that shook his self-confidence and made him stare admiringly at the rest of the prisoners.

There were words like 'pragmatism', 'demagogy', 'capitalism', 'communism', 'socialism', 'compradorism'. What was it all about? What did it mean? Get ready for some more lies, Hani. Get ready for some other things you won't understand. Like 'compradorism'. Yes, your father's a comprador, Hani. He's merely a means to channel in goods from the capitalist countries. That's why he has no problem marketing goods from Israel. Your father, Hani, is a reactionary. He's only interested in safe profit, and cares nothing for the country's welfare. It's true that not all the bourgeoisie were like that. The European bourgeoisie provided leadership. They were pioneering and progressive; not comprador. No, I don't claim that my father's better than yours – God's curse on both their beards. But listen to

124

me. You like the name Abu al-Izz? Well, it'll never be yours, even if you try to buy it with ten bottles of cola, two bars of chocolate and a tin of tuna fish! My goodness! What an appetite you get! How hungry can you be! I wish I hadn't eaten my egg this morning.

The others listened as Salih spoke: 'Who's responsible for the country's lack of industrialization? Who's to blame for the backwardness of the workers? They lack confidence and technical skills; they have no true sense of national identity. And who's responsible? This is a question that demands an answer, no matter how much the truth may hurt. You are to blame. Yes, you, you and you, and her, and me above all others. But it's not enough just to admit "I'm responsible" to expiate your guilt and find peace. The problem goes deeper than that. We must read, plan, act. We must turn our backs on the past and look to the future! The occupation won't last for ever. That's certain. And when it's over, what will the workers do? They're not peasants, merchants and small artisans any more. Because of the situation we're in, everybody's had to become a common labourer. So what will we do with them when the occupation's over? The oil wealth's all sitting in the banks of Europe, stimulating trade and industry there, not here. Europe becomes prosperous while we stay as we are. The wealth must be distributed equitably. We must industrialize before time runs out. The oil reserves won't last for ever. And then what? Then what, I ask you.

Well, Hani, come and listen, thought Basil. That's a solid education, to be sure. But I wonder where Salih gets all those words? Not too difficult. He copies them out of books; I could do the same. I'll start tomorrow, and see if I can't explore all the big words the way he does – communism, socialism, imperialism, demagogy, compradorism . . . Ha, ha, ha! Compradorism! I've got your number, Haj Abdullah! By God, it's perfectly legal to steal from someone like you. Your crates of cola had better beware of my devilish plans! And your nuts, the lovely

125

pistachios, and the roast chick-peas! Oh, how your stomach can rumble! Oh mother! A bowl of soup would be sweeter right now than Suad Husni's legs.* How lovely girls are; when you see one walk by, the earth and sky seem to dance. Thank heaven for masturbation. Well, they said I'd become a man; I'll prove it as soon as I get out of here. The country's full of factory girls. And they sure know how to dance.

* Suad Husni is a well-known actress.

126

The soldier opened the door of cell 23 and Zuhdi came in, carrying five blankets, a couple of bowls and a plastic mug. All eyes turned curiously towards him. But no one greeted him. They simply stared at him suspiciously.

Zuhdi felt terribly alienated, a sensation worse than the loneliness he'd felt during his five days of solitary confinement. 'He works in Israel,' someone whispered. The words exploded in his ear like a bomb and his blood boiled. They don't realize I'm worth more than any of them, that I split Shlomo's head open with a wrench. They're here just because they shouted in demonstrations and mouthed a few slogans, like Basil and Hamada. He looked around anxiously. Maybe Hamada would be in this very cell. But how could he still be in prison? Impossible. Adil wouldn't bail his brother Basil out and leave Hamada for want of a guarantor.

The cell was packed; the men sat around in loose circles. He knew some of the faces but no one seemed to recognize him. Zuhdi dumped his blankets on the floor. He sat in the middle of the room for over an hour. No one spoke to him. His spirits sank.

What's going on? Doesn't anybody care about me? Even the Jews didn't act like this. Their blows, their interrogations, were easier to take than this terrible indifference. At least with them you still had some sense of worth, of being a man, of having important information Israel was trying to get at. Then he'd been able to revel in his defiance, to stare back challengingly and with contempt at his interrogator. All that gave a man a sense of importance. But now! Now there was no challenge at all, no interrogation, no blows, nothing.

Shortly before dinner time an older man, perhaps in his fifties, came up to him. In a rural accent he asked whether Zuhdi was from the city or the countryside. When Zuhdi said that he came from town, the man turned away to a backgammon game. After a few moments Zuhdi swallowed his pride and tapped the man on the shoulder with his uninjured hand: 'And you, where are you from?'

Without so much as lifting his gaze from the board, the man replied, 'From north Asira. Why?'

'You asked me, so I asked you. Is that a crime?'

The man didn't answer, but went on watching the movements of the pieces across the board.

Dinner arrived. Two of the prisoners went round the room, filling the bowls with soup. Others poured out the tea. Zuhdi sat apart from the groups of men, who sat round in circles joking and laughing with one another. He ate alone, wondering, Why are they ostracizing me? Aren't these men Arabs like myself? Or rather, aren't I an Arab like them? Working in Israel doesn't mean being Israel's agent. Don't they understand that? They took away my work permit; how else can I eat? Who'd feed Saadiyya and the children? He ate without appetite, forcing the food down. If these people treat me like this when I'm here with them in prison, he thought, how will they treat me when I'm on the outside? How cruel they are! Even Shlomo wasn't as cruel as this. He had a sudden memory of the man on the ground, his head split open, his eyes staring upwards, and he felt regret and a deep sense of guilt. Shlomo wasn't bad. He knew that now.

The meal was over. Three big men came over to Zuhdi. One of them, who seemed shrewd and intelligent, began to question him while the other two listened. When did they take you in? What for? Do you belong to any organization? Why did you hit Shlomo? What did they ask you? What did you tell them? Show us the marks of torture on your body. Zuhdi, annoyed, replied gruffly. Finally he blurted out, 'What is this? I'm not a spy! Stop asking such stupid questions!'

The three men moved away. Zuhdi, watching them out of the corner of his eye, noticed that the intelligent one sat down in the far corner of the cell, took out a notebook and began writing something down.

Next morning the procedure was repeated. Two other men came over and started asking him the same questions. When did they take you in? What for? Why did you hit Shlomo? What did the interrogator ask, and what did you tell him?

'I'm not a spy, you guys!' he yelled again. 'Why are you treating me like this?'

The two men withdrew, but one went over to the intelligent man who'd questioned him the evening before and whispered to him. More notes. In the afternoon the old villager came over to him and asked the same questions. Zuhdi flushed. He started screaming at the old man, threatening to split his head open just as he had Shlomo's. The villager blinked in surprise, and said hesitantly, 'I was only trying to be friendly; why are you so angry with me?' To show his good intentions, he produced a crumpled letter from his pocket. 'Could you read this letter for me, please?' he asked Zuhdi politely. 'I don't know how to read.'

'Hasn't anybody read it to you yet?' asked Zuhdi uneasily.

'Oh yes,' said the old man, 'they've read it to me three times already, but I haven't had my fill of it. Every time I hear what it says, it all comes back to me. Please read it to me.'

Zuhdi began the letter, with its news of the village, while the old man sighed and shook his head.

'. . . and we'd like you to know that Masouda's given

birth to a white calf . . .'

Zuhdi's eyes opened wide. 'Masouda's given birth to a calf?'

'Masouda's the cow. Go on.'

As Zuhdi read on, he smiled for the first time since he'd been in prison: 'We're delighted to tell you that your daughter-in-law Munira's had a boy. We've named him after you.'

The peasant nodded proudly. 'A boy at last, after five girls,' he said. 'Would you believe it? Do you have any children?'

'Yes.'

'Well, at last,' smiled the peasant, 'at last there's a boy to carry on my name. Thanks be to God that I lived to see the day.'

'Your name's Mahmoud, right?'

'Yes, but they call me Abu Salim. If I was home I'd have slaughtered a lamb in honour of the baby. Can you go on, please? Tell me again about the aubergines and the tomatoes.'

Zuhdi went on reading, enjoying the letter. 'We've planted some aubergines,' he read, 'but wish we hadn't. The price they fetch on the market isn't anything like it was last year.'

'Yes,' the peasant said sadly, 'Israeli aubergines have taken over the market. How can we compete with them? Go on, go on, finish it.'

'The tomatoes fetched a good price, but not enough to make up for our losses on the aubergines.'

'Ah, Salim.' The peasant shook his head sorrowfully. 'God help you. You've got your mother, your brother's wife, your daughters and now a son, the land, Masouda and her calf to care for. I don't know how you'll manage.'

'God protect him; it'll be all right,' said Zuhdi, thinking of his own wife, Saadiyya, and his children. After a moment's silence, he asked, 'Did they treat you like they're treating me when you first arrived in prison?'

130

'Oh no, just the opposite,' said the old man. 'They held a party for me. You see, I had friends here and they introduced me, so the others trusted me.'

Zuhdi stared hard at him: 'What are you trying to say – "they trusted me"? Don't they trust me, then?'

The peasant frowned. 'How would I know?' he said.

For Zuhdi this was the last straw. He grabbed the old man by the scruff of the neck and shook him violently. 'Don't know, eh?' he repeated. 'What do you mean, you don't know. You mean I'm a spy? I'll shake the living hell out of you!'

Hands seized Zuhdi, trying to break his grip on the old man, but he held on, yelling, 'You bastard! Me a spy! I'll kill you!'

He felt a big arm encircle his neck from behind. This made him even more furious. He released the old man and spun to face the others. He grabbed the empty soup tureen and waved it menacingly at them. He had lost all control.

'You're plotting against me, you bastards! I'm telling you, I'm not leaving till I've killed someone! Come on! If any of you are men, come over here!'

Some of the prisoners stood around watching him closely; others simply remained sitting, observing the scene in silence. Zuhdi could feel eyes upon him from all sides. He moved forward, blinded by rage, and spoke to one of the men: 'Come on! You think you're pretty sharp, eh? Well, show me something!'

The man backed off toward the wall. Zuhdi shouted at another prisoner, daring him to fight. But he too drew back and crouched near the wall. Zuhdi was now charging back and forth across the room, oblivious of the dishes on the floor. Like a child in a tantrum, he kicked the cups and bowls and trampled on the mats. He went over to the small shelf of books against the wall, and hurled them to the ground, throwing some at the men staring at him and some at the windows that had been blocked up with bricks and mortar.

'Take this! And this! What's the matter with you? I'm no spy, you bastards!'

The intelligent-looking man came up to him, speaking calmly and holding out his hand in apparent friendship. 'Calm down, old fellow. What's the matter?'

'What's the matter?' repeated Zuhdi. 'What's the matter with *you*? There's nothing wrong with me, I'm a hundred per cent okay. You think I don't understand your games?'

'Calm down, man,' repeated the other. 'Calm down! And shake the hand I'm offering you.'

'I won't shake anybody's hand,' insisted Zuhdi furiously. 'I'll go on like this until you see that your plots against me won't work. You think I don't know your games? Here, take this!'

He flung a heavy book against the far wall. Its binding split, and the pages flew apart and scattered over the floor; the prisoners' eyes shifted from the fluttering pages to the big man raging like a bull. The hand, however, remained stretched out toward him.

'Come on, let's shake hands! We're all brothers here. Come on! My name's Adil, what's yours?'

The name Adil made him sad and he was overwhelmed by longing for his friend. What a difference between this Adil and the one he knew so well!

'Come on, my friend, shake hands! We're all brothers here.'

'Brothers! I saw what kind of brothers you are when you left me sitting alone on my mat for over an hour. You just let me sit there like a mangy dog and didn't even offer me one word of welcome.'

'Okay, okay. Blame me. It's my fault. But let's shake hands.'

Adil came forward and gave Zuhdi a hug. Then he took him by the arm, led him over to a corner and sat him down, smiling and continuing to speak in a polite, friendly voice.

'Welcome. You're welcome here. How come you're so upset, my friend?'

Zuhdi sat on a mattress and rested his back against the wall, still breathing hard. His rage melted away as rapidly as it had risen, and he felt like crying. But he controlled himself and swore silently as he mopped his brow. Then, almost unconsciously, the words came pouring out: 'Well, who did I leave Saadiyya and the children for then? And who did I split Shlomo's head open for? Who did I suffer their beatings for? They put me in a strait-jacket that practically made my eyes pop out! Prison may be bad, but you guys are worse. I'm sick of the whole lot of it – Jews, Arabs, the factory, the work permit I lost, the sandstorms of Kuwait! I don't . . . well, I don't even know my head from my foot any more. Are you treating me like this because I'm just a poor working man and you guys all read books? You think I'm illiterate? Well, I'm not. Give me your fattest book and I'll read the most difficult page in it for you. Come on, give me a book, mister! Come on!'

Adil was picking up the scattered pages and trying to put them in order. Suddenly Zuhdi snatched a sheet from him and tore it in two, leaving half in Adil's hand. Zuhdi began to read from his half in a strange high-pitched voice. The prisoners listened, trying to hide their smiles. Mahmoud the peasant sat on a mattress looking confused and uncomprehending, while Zuhdi went on loudly, mispronouncing words and ignoring grammar and punctuation. Gradually his reading slowed, his voice dropped; finally he stopped. He put the sheet of paper in his lap and stared defiantly at the faces gazing at him. After a while he picked up the half sheet of paper in his lap and smoothed out the creases. He held it out to Adil, who took it without comment and calmly placed it back in the book.

'What,' he asked Zuhdi patiently, 'did you get from what you read?'

'Nothing at all,' replied Zuhdi with childlike truthfulness. Then his pride and defiance returned and he stretched out a hand to take the book back from Adil: 'Give it back,' he said. 'I'll read it slowly, then I'll understand

133

what it says.'

'No,' said Adil. 'It takes time. This is a hard book. But I'll give you one you'll enjoy. Have you read anything by Naguib Mahfouz?'*

'Who's he?'

'Okay, I'll give you a book by Naguib Mahfouz, something you'll like. Do you read stories?'

'Well, I listen to stories,' answered Zuhdi. 'Abu Sabir used to tell me everything he read – tales of Abu Zayd, of Antar and Abla, Hasan the Clever. Abu Sabir's my neighbour and my friend. He sliced his fingers off with the blade of a saw. Then the bastards refused to give him first aid. But why should I be telling you all this? You tell me. Why do you treat people this way? Leaving me on my mat like a dog for hours without one word of welcome. A lot of ridiculous questions that I answered once, twice, three times. And still you weren't happy. Isn't the interrogation over yet? First I get interrogated by the Jews, then by the Arabs! I swear I don't know what to say any more.'

Adil nodded in agreement. 'Yes, you're quite right,' he said. 'Please forgive us. But we had good reason. You'll understand in a little while. Come on fellows, let's throw a party for Zuhdi.'

The prisoners collected the dishes and straightened out the room. Then they sat down in a circle, leaving a small empty space in the middle. Adil conferred in a whisper with some of the men and Zuhdi watched them with anxious curiosity. Adil stood up and made an announcement that Zuhdi did not understand. This made him even more suspicious and he was determined to defend himself if necessary.

Some of the younger prisoners sat close to the door and began to shake their backgammon boards like tambourines. The cell echoed to the sound of drumming on empty buckets, singing and clapping, and one man started

* Naguib Mahfouz: a contemporary Egyptian novelist, considered one of the great modern Arab authors.

dancing, moving and shaking his body frenetically. Zuhdi sat staring in amazement at the madness all around him. This was some party!

Some soldiers came up to the door and yelled, 'What's going on?'

No one replied, but the noise grew louder, boards banging and buckets being beaten. The soldiers covered their ears and moved away from the door. The din now grew even louder, so deafening that Zuhdi began yelling at them to stop. But no one heard him or paid any attention. Then he saw them drag a man out and push him into a corner. Two burly men rolled up their sleeves and started hitting him. He screamed in pain, but the screams were drowned in the continuing uproar of the insane celebration. The beating went on for a quarter of an hour. The man's eyes were bruised he was covered in blood; he sank to the ground, being kicked from all directions.

'You're going to kill him!' shouted Zuhdi. He tried to get up and help the man, but hands restrained him. Meanwhile Adil looked on approvingly at what was happening. Finally the man was picked up and flung down near Zuhdi and Adil. The prisoners made a tight circle round him. The noise had died down: the interrogation was about to begin. Adil began reading from some papers: contradictory statements the man himself had made. Adil pointed out the inconsistencies and advised him to confess: 'You're co-operating with them. It's perfectly clear. For how long? Since when? Speak up!'

The man began to confess, while Zuhdi listened. His heart thumped. Then his confusion cleared. The man was a spy! At last he understood!

Zuhdi developed severe constipation. His new friends advised him to eat more vegetables, especially lettuce; they teased him by prescribing one fruit and vegetable after another, until his eyes flashed and he threatened to use his iron fists on them if they didn't stop their silliness. He watched them beginning their evening exercises, racing around like sprites, and began to feel that his head was caught in a vice, throbbing. He threw Naguib Mahfouz's novel *Midaq Alley* aside and withdrew to a far corner of the room, confused and unwell. He sat watching the prisoners, sweat pouring off them, oblivious to him while they exercised. Mahmoud the old peasant was sitting next to the Syrian guerrilla, who was regaling him once more with the news of Masouda and her white calf. From time to time Adil glanced pensively at the young men racing about, before burying himself once again in his books and papers. Zuhdi was lonely, turned his face to the wall to hide his tears. Where were Saadiyya and the children? Where was Hamada? Had he been released from prison or was he still nesting there, like a young pigeon with broken wings? And what of Adil, and Abu Sabir? Did the songs of Farid al-Atrash still resound through the town square? And what about the clashing of the cymbals which announced the seller of liquorice and carob drinks and mingled with the recorded voice of Abd al-Basit Abd al-Samad chanting verses from the Koran? While he mused, his city seemed to acquire colour and clarity. Everything there was beautiful, he thought, even the barrels of stinking fish. But in prison everything was drab, dismal, cold. This Adil wasn't like the other Adil, though both talked about the same things. This Adil was too divorced from people, too busy with his books. How could any heart stir with emotion without knowing the warmth of life? The other Adil didn't speak very much, but even his silence was eloquent; other people spoke only when they opened their mouths. Yes, Adil al-Karmi was something different, something fine, bigger than the headaches, the stomach pains and the loneliness. And what about Saadiyya and the children, with their ever-open mouths? Who'd look after them, who'd feed them? If I stay in prison much longer, it's goodbye to Saadiyya's gold bracelets. Never mind, Saadiyya; I'll buy you some more. Don't turn up your nose like that! It makes you look like a monkey! I've told you that a thousand times. I didn't buy those bracelets just so you could decorate your pretty wrists. No, gold bracelets have other uses, uses that are fully appreciated only when you're in prison. They're your savings bank, one that's proved its value even more now that the banks themselves are useless. What can the banks do against the occupation army? How can they resist? If the special Koranic verses can't 'save' us, what hope is there for our worn-out people? Chant on, Abd al-Basit! Say the verse: 'I put my trust in the Lord of the people.' But what about people like me whose heads and stomachs won't listen? I've got no enthusiasm for 'resistance' when I'm so constipated. It reminds me of lentils and the Woman's Hour programme. Long live lentils, Saadiyya! Even lentils seem precious to me these days!

The young prisoners were weight-lifting. They'd made the weights from concrete set in empty plastic containers. They raised and lowered them with great care, like a father holding his little son, the only one among ten daughters. When they went outside for the exercise periods they wrapped the weights in blankets, and Sabri hid them behind the infirmary door on the mornings of inspection days. The damn soldiers were always searching, their eyes looking out for anything that might be forbidden or disallowed, anything except sodomy or spying. But Adil and his companions kept a close look-out for any deviant behaviour, whether sexual or moral. Mahmoud the peasant, for example, was found guilty of taking more than his share of soup. A disciplinary council was convened and the Syrian guerrilla was asked to carry out the sentence. When he proved reluctant to do so, both men got a beating during a 'celebration', to the accompaniment of rattling dishes and banging backgammon boards. A government within a government. Adil sat at the head of the government of cell number 23, claiming to be the 'conscience' of the Palestinian revolution! But what a cold heart the man had!

I'm afraid that power will make him become like all the rest, Zuhdi thought. He'll give the orders and we'll have to carry them out. History repeats itself, adopting fine, resounding names – democracy, socialism, the proletariat. Then someone like Stalin raises his sickle and harvests millions of necks, while the masses go on screaming and whistling for the lord of might and power, singing the praises of Moscow and communist China. Adil al-Karmi, my friend, my greetings and respects go out to you; now I understand what you were talking about.

This damned colic! And Saadiyya's bracelets will soon be gone. From now on there'll be no more people listening carefully to Woman's Hour. Or to Abd al-Basit, or Farid al-Atrash. In the centre of town the buildings will grow taller and the people smaller. The more gigantic the buildings, the more dwarfed the pedestrians look. Buildings rise, while the earth and those who walk upon it shrink. Adil's evening sessions explain things in a way that's difficult for people like me with stomach pains to comprehend. And *Midaq Alley* is only a path that leads to another Mahfouz novel, *A Beginning and an End*. The backs of dry books stare out from high shelves and only the educated can reach the top. My hands are good for nothing but wielding pliers and wrenches, and all I can think of is a green salad swimming in oil. One spoonful of castor oil does more good than all the slogans and explanations in Adil's head.

Adil came over to him. 'What's up, Zuhdi? Still worrying about Saadiyya and the kids? Forget about it, man. You're still just at the beginning of the road.'

'Forget!' cried Zuhdi. 'How can a man forget his own flesh and blood? And how Saadiyya cooks vegetables so beautifully that people ought to bow down before her?'

'Come off it, Zuhdi,' Adil said. 'You've seen what it means to the petty bourgeoisie to have properly pressed trousers. They're more concerned about the creases in their trousers than they are about their sisters' virtue. The bourgeoisie have condemned themselves by condemning their victims. This country's filled with trash. And you and I, Zuhdi, are going to be part of the clean-up team.'

Oh, now I celebrate your memory, Adil al-Karmi, my brother! Did you hear what he said? He's going to make me a member of a clean-up crew! Should I accept? Cleaning? – you can't clean up without dirtying your hands. I'm afraid these hands of mine will get too used to the curse of dirt and make a profession out of weeding.

Shlomo's head's split open, blood discolouring his face, that face that so often expressed hatred and distaste. But Shlomo wasn't all bad. He was just a human being, like you and me. But he was also an ass, just like the thousands of Shlomos before him. I'm an ass too. Two asses fighting over a bundle of clover and a pack-saddle made in a factory. And what did we gain from it all? He's in the hospital and I'm in prison. While the factory goes on producing and the people continue consuming. And the Shalom building keeps growing higher, the West Bank bellies get fatter, and Radio Israel repeats its anthem about Jerusalem the Golden. Fairouz* sings on for the rose of all cities, Jerusalem. And I just sit here. Yes, I'm here and you're there,

* Fairouz is a popular Lebanese singer one of whose best-known songs is about Jerusalem.

139

Shlomo. Each of us wearing a pack-saddle made in a factory, and talking nothing but nonsense mixed with slogans.

This Adil tells me, 'One's life is expendable in the cause of one's country.' For the cause of one's life, the country's expendable! You said that. Marx said it. Was it you or was it Marx? I can't remember. My stomachache makes my head hurt and my headache makes my stomach hurt. The two have come together, and my constipation has become a common denominator, uniting two opposites. Food, a bed, a woman. Saadiyya's thighs shine in my memory like the sands of Haifa harbour. And here I sit in prison, listening to heroic anthems and squirming with desire for a dish of hot lentil soup! While Adil goes on repeating his maxims and his advice. Get off my back, Adil! All your books and explanations aren't worth a spoonful of castor oil!'

The Syrian guerrilla asked him, 'How're you feeling?'

'Rotten.'

'Come on then, we'll make you a nice cup of tea and have you feeling better. Give us the two buckets, Abu Salim.'

The two men prepared the primitive cooker while Zuhdi watched, his hands folded across his stomach. Two buckets were set facing one another. Then two bits of string were threaded through holes in the sides of the empty jam tin and it was suspended from a broom handle between the buckets. Then they filled the tin with water, shredded an egg box into small pieces, placed the shreds beneath the tin and lit them.

'Hey, save the next round for us,' yelled a group leader from the far corner.

'Are you making some for me too?' asked Adil.

'Of course,' replied the Syrian generously.

Zuhdi began sipping the hot tea noisily, while the other inmates looked on enviously.

'Come on, Zuhdi,' said the Syrian, trying to cheer him up. 'What's wrong with you? Say something, man. Talking about it will make you feel better. From the looks of you I'd say you're not just constipated. You're lonely. Come on, it'll be all right. Tomorrow's visiting day, maybe you'll see your family. Not like me; five years without seeing anyone.'

Zuhdi was silent.

Mahmoud the peasant broke in. 'Shall I tell you the latest news about Masouda, Zuhdi? The white calf died. God damn this bad luck! That's the third calf to die less than a month after birth. I don't know what's wrong with that damn cow. The calves look great when they're born, but then they die. I hope you don't have such bad luck in your life.'

But no one answered, and Mahmoud too fell silent, staring at his reflection in the surface of the tea. After a moment, he went on, 'Tomorrow I'm going to shave before visiting time. Otherwise my wife won't give me the chicken and onions she's bringing; that's what she threatened last time.'

The Syrian's face lit up. 'Chicken and onions?' he cried. 'Oh, Abu Salim, my friend, you won't forget me, will you?'

'Forget you, are you crazy? All alone, far from your own country, with no relatives or family at all? How could I forget you? You're our best mate. My wife promised she'd bring you a chicken all to yourself. But you know the rules in this cell – Adil gets everything and distributes it to everyone else, mouthful by mouthful.'

Adil nodded. 'Yes,' he said seriously. 'Just as I also distribute portions of all the others' food to you. That's socialism.'

Abu Salim tapped Zuhdi on the shoulder, whispering, 'He's after us with his socialism and capitalism even when all we want is to eat chicken and onions! I don't know!'

The men began to sip the tea, each gazing down at his reflection in the cup. The Syrian, his voice trembling with longing, asked, 'What do you see in your cups?'

'I can see my wife near the bread oven,' said Zuhdi. 'Her sleeves are rolled up and the sweat's pouring from her

141

forehead. Her hands are busy with the dough, dividing it up into round loaves and putting them on the burning hot baking-stone. What about you? What can you see?'

'I see the face of a child I don't know,' the Syrian replied. 'They say he's my son. His name's Nidal. I imagine his cheek with a red birthmark the size of a mulberry. He must have one. It's an old story, one I've never forgotten. We were out walking in the Salihiyya quarter in Damascus, and my wife, Izdihar, was in the first months of her pregnancy. A tall mulberry tree hung over the path from behind the wall of a villa. It was the red Damascene variety. Izdihar asked me to pick her a berry, so the child wouldn't have a birthmark on his face to spoil his appearance. So I picked up a stone and threw it at the tree. At that moment, the owner of the villa peered out from behind the wall and began swearing at me. Izdihar took my hand and said that it wasn't worth fighting over a berry.'

'I see,' commented Adil, frowning. 'This story illustrates many things. You're here in prison now for the sake of that man who owned the mulberry tree and the villa. You offered your life to defend his interests, whereas he begrudged you a single mulberry. Do you see what I mean?'

The Syrian said nothing, but continued to gaze dreamily at the images in his teacup. 'Now I see Izdihar's face. I fell in love with her at first sight. I used to pass her house on my way to work – I must have gone that way for years without noticing her. One day I was walking under the stairs to her house when suddenly I felt some drops of cold water on my head. I shouted up the stairs and when I looked up I could see her milk-white thighs. She was carrying a straw broom in one hand and a bucket of water in the other. Her hair was tied up with a red ribbon and I remember noticing that she had a shiny gold tooth. "I beg your pardon," she said, in a voice like a dove cooing. "Next time keep your eyes open." My eyes were already wide open gazing up at those white thighs, so I shouted back: "My eyes are wide open. But you look too and see what you've done." And then our eyes met: it was just like a flash of electricity! Eyes like a gazelle, she had, with gorgeous long lashes. God in heaven! And when she smiled, I couldn't help yelling: "Pour the rest of the water over me, and I'll be damned if I ever move!" She burst out laughing, it was music to my ears. After that I kept passing by her house, going to work and coming home, and every time our eyes would light up and flash like bolts of lightning or the firing of Katyushas.'

Zudhi smiled, moved by the story. The Syrian went on contemplating the images inside his cup.

'Yes, then we got married. And she got pregnant. When they chose me for the resistance operation, I told her she should call the child in her womb Nidal, "struggle". So that's what she'll have called him.'

Adil interrupted. 'Yes,' he said grimly, 'the "struggle" of the downtrodden classes.'

No one seemed to hear him, so immersed were they in their memories, oblivious to Adil and his political explanations.

'The Red Cross promised they'd work things out with the authorities,' the Syrian went on. 'They may let my folks visit me. But it's been years and I'm still waiting. I can't believe they'll come, yet I go on hoping they might. If I didn't have that hope, my life would be as miserable as your face, Zuhdi!'

Zuhdi smiled and shook his head. 'Look, I'm smiling!' he said. 'Does that cheer you up?'

Then he stood up and announced the good news: 'I think it's on the way!' he cried.

And off he raced to the toilet.

Zuhdi glanced furtively at the man next to him. Abu Nidal's nicotine-stained fingers were trembling and the small pair of scissors in his hand was shaking. Zuhdi decided to try and cheer his friend up. 'I'll tell you a dirty joke, Abu Nidal.'

'Go ahead,' replied the Syrian without enthusiasm.

Zuhdi himself roared with laughter throughout the joke, but Abu Nidal only smiled politely, his thoughts clearly far away. The prisoners laughed loud and long when Zuhdi had finished; Abu Nidal merely pretended to smile. Zuhdi was seized by bitterness and remorse. Here I am laughing, while he's wretched and depressed. We at least see our friends and relatives, but he doesn't even have the reassurance of knowing his wife and children are all right. And tomorrow's his son's birthday. He's five now, and knows nothing of his father except his good reputation. And the man has fits of silent depression. I know, I've often woken up at night and seen him hiding his tears beneath the blankets, his head turned towards the wall. He's an expert at hiding his emotions in public. Recently he seems to have become thinner and paler. He's beginning to give up hope; the promises made by the Red Cross no longer cheer him up.

He went on stealing glances at his friend, who was trying to thread the needle of his sewing machine. But his hand shook so much he couldn't manage it, and he asked Zuhdi for help. 'It's my eyes, I've got bad eyesight,' he explained. Zuhdi threaded the needle, then went on sewing the pocket to the shirt, whispering as he did so, 'I'm giving up smoking. I'm going to join the sports team to tone up my muscles.'

'Oh, and who's going to get the cigarettes you earn then?' asked the Syrian, suddenly interested.

'You can have them,' Zuhdi whispered, his expression serious, 'but don't tell anyone.'

He looked to make sure no one had overheard. But the others seemed too busy with their sewing machines to notice him or his neighbour. Someone made an important announcement: 'News has reached us from the kitchen that they're going to give us stuffed courgettes!'

'Stuffed courgettes!'

'Tell us another!'

'They'd never do that. It'd be a disaster. If they wanted to give each inmate one courgette, the cooks would have to hollow out eight hundred courgettes – or more. And that's just if the operation's restricted to the Nablus prison. If they wanted to include all the prisoners on the West Bank, in Gaza and inside Israel, they'd have to devote the entire machinery of the state to this vital task of stuffing courgettes. If the news is true, friends, we should rejoice and celebrate the collapse of the state budget.'

'Don't be so quick to celebrate,' commented someone else, who was busy with the sleeves of a shirt. If the news is true, they'll use all their technology for the task. They might have machines that can hollow out fifty courgettes a second! In that case, they won't need to mobilize all the machinery of the state to provide the promised meal.'

'You always were a defeatist,' chimed in another in disgust. 'You're always putting us down. Leave us a little hope, friend. Is there anything wrong with that?'

'It's ridiculous for the defeated like us to continue to hope.'

'Okay,' Zuhdi interjected, 'that does it! From now on

no more cigarettes for you.'

The man charged with defeatism raised his head from his sewing and smiled. 'You made up your mind about that before you heard what I said, Zuhdi. Why use my defeatist attitude to help justify the promise you made to your friend?'

The two men stared hard at one another. Then Zuhdi let out a loud guffaw: 'So you overheard our conversation you bastard!' He nudged his neighbour and commented: 'Hear that, Abu Nidal? These devils don't miss a damned trick!'

Someone observed with pride, 'Being imprisoned has many advantages. The most important is that it teaches you to watch what you say, and to sharpen your ears to hear everything that goes on around you, even in the toilets!'

This was greeted with a chorus of laughter, and Zuhdi joined in. Then he understood the full point of the joke, and said, 'Say what you mean, big mouth!'

'Oh, I don't mean anything more than I said. Don't blame me for what others think.'

'Wriggled your way out of that neatly, didn't you, you bastard? Fair enough. So what if I promised to give him my cigarettes? Is that a crime?'

'Absolutely not. But why didn't you announce it publicly? Socialism doesn't deprive you of the freedom of disposing of what's distributed to you in any way you like. For example, you're free to dispose of your courgette just as you wish. You can eat it. Or frame it. Or embalm it. You're free. Just as you're free to give it to me, and I'm free to accept your present. And from now on I intend to repay you faithfully.'

Everyone roared with laughter, Abu Nidal included. Zuhdi shook his head sorrowfully. 'God protect me from these devils!' he cried. 'How can I compete when they all think they're as big as Ben Gurion himself?'

'Israel should beware of what it's created – a time bomb about to explode. Its prisons have become breeding grounds for ideas, not disposal sites for land-mines.

History will find it hard to judge whether the occupation was a blessing or a disaster. It's a tough question.'

Zuhdi left the sewing workshop with his eight cigarettes and stood in the sunny prison courtyard, waiting to fulfil his promise to Abu Nidal. Although the sight of the cigarettes excited his craving for them, he controlled himself and determined to stick by his decision, if only for three days. He'd got himself into a fix, and he'd have to take the consequences. A man's word is sharper than the blade of a sword. He reminded himself wrily of the proverb that a man gets tripped up by the tongue, not the leg. But when he saw the two Israeli guards at the iron gates of the prison lighting up their cigarettes, he couldn't resist taking one himself. What did it matter if Abu Nidal got seven cigarettes, instead of eight? Could he ever have dreamed of such a treasure, anyway? The sun was hot. Leaning against the trunk of a tree made him think of life outside, of freedom. Images from the outside world flowed through his mind in quick succession, especially of his daily journey to Tel Aviv . . .

In the early morning the city is always shrouded in mist. On the bus our heads are heavy with sleep. On the hills outside Tulkarm the breeze we feel is perfumed with the scent of orange blossom. And the eucalyptus trees in the Khadouri School glisten like the sails of God in the heavens above Carmel. And then there's the voice of Adil al-Karmi, so pleasing to the ear, filling our heads with thoughts of compassion and dreams of brotherhood. God's peace be upon you, Adil al-Karmi! Come and teach these people here how love can be mightier than all sorrow. But what would become of Adil if he had to undergo the terrible experience of prison life? Would he keep the same nobility of spirit, the same love?

Zuhdi lit his cigarette and inhaled deeply. He was looking towards the door leading to the main prison gate when he saw the guards open the door to reveal a child no more than five years old. The boy raced into the open courtyard and stood still in the middle, looking around, obviously searching for the face of one particular man. Then he ran towards Zuhdi.

'Are you my daddy?' he asked, panting.

The cigarette slipped from Zuhdi's fingers and his heart began to pound. The words stuck in his throat, and he looked in confusion towards the other men there, but their eyes were focused on two women standing just inside the door.

'Are you my daddy?' the boy demanded again.

His head swimming, Zudhi stretched out his hand: 'Are you Nidal?' he asked.

The child hurled himself into Zuhdi's arms, crying and sobbing: 'Daddy! Daddy!'

Zuhdi hugged the small trembling body close to his own, his tears flowing. The other men all stared at the child in confusion and some headed back to their cells, unable to see any more. Others, weeping silently, turned to face the walls of the courtyard. The two women, accompanied by an Israeli officer, were now approaching, wiping their eyes with handkerchiefs as they came.

Zuhdi looked at the two soldiers guarding the door. They were weeping, too. So you shed tears, then? The barbarity and torture you witness in the prison walls doesn't make you cry, but a boy no more than five does?

The Syrian rushed out of the sewing workshop, snatched the child from Zuhdi's embrace and burst into tears. The road of tears is long, longer than the road of struggle. Izdihar stood behind the child, wiping her eyes; the grandmother, draped in black, would have dropped to the ground had the men not held her up. A prisoner suddenly gave a great shout of joy: 'God is most great, my friends! Long live Palestine, Arab and free!'

The silent and dismal courtyard soon echoed with the shouts of many men: 'Long live Palestine, Arab and free!'

The two soldiers wiped away their tears, locked the door from the outside and disappeared behind barriers of reinforced concrete.

When Adil dropped by the shop he found Basil there as usual, sitting with his two friends and telling them how he'd put the military governor's neck out of joint all by himself. That, of course, had been during his historic arrest. Adil stood at the door of the shop.

'How long are you going to keep this up, Basil?' he asked. 'What about your studies? There's only a few weeks before the exams, so when are you going to start working? Didn't you waste enough time in prison?'

Basil seized upon the word prison. 'You're always going on about prison,' he complained. 'Morning and evening, day and night. Always reminding me of prison and its woes. Am I responsible for being put into prison? Or the imprisonment of the other men like me? No sir! Certainly not. No way am I responsible for the actions and interests of the occupation. And the terrors I witnessed are part of my national duty.'

Adil smiled, looking quizzically at his brother. 'Who are you trying to kid?' he asked, but Basil pretended not to hear him, and went on talking.

'Inside they told me that prison was for men. And that those who don't go to prison, even for a day, will never become real men, even if they grow two moustaches rather than one.'

One of the boys asked maliciously, 'And has your father been to prison or not?'

The young men laughed, including Basil.

'But what about your studies, boys?' Adil persisted.

'Hey, we're not boys any more,' objected Hani.

'Okay. You're young men. But men mustn't shirk their responsibilities, and at the moment you're responsible for your studies; are you studying?'

'I've *been* studying,' replied Hani, turning to look at the till.

The others echoed his words, one of them insisting that he'd prepared all his work for the coming week. Adil shook his head in disbelief. 'Come on, Basil, off to your studies,' he said.

'I've finished.'

'When? You haven't opened a book since the day you came out of prison.'

Basil turned to the other boys. 'If I don't want to get out of bed in the morning,' he complained, 'my sister Nuwar says: "You've forgotten the time you spent in prison." And if I don't want to eat something, my mother says: "Too bad you haven't got that prison rubbish to eat!" And if I'm slow in doing what my father wants, he says: "Why did you bother to come out of prison?" When will you all learn? I'm not responsible for my imprisonment, nor for any prison sentences I may get in the future.'

He glanced around to see the effect of his words and realized that the audience expected something more. He opened his mouth to speak again but Adil silenced him with an angry stare.

'Off you go, pronto!' he said.

Then he turned away, leaving Basil in a difficult position.

'Better go, Basil,' advised one of the boys. 'Best to avoid trouble.'

'But who does he think he is,' protested Basil, 'My keeper? Isn't it enough to have my father order me about? By God, I'm not going!'

Then he continued, insolently, 'The most cultured man in prison was a mere illiterate labourer who couldn't read a word.'

'Well, don't you believe me?' he demanded, staring uneasily at the others.

One boy asked him, 'But what about Salih and Elias? Antun and Hamza?'

'They don't know what the real revolution's all about,' Basil answered contemptuously. 'True revolutionaries don't carry books. They carry weapons! Daggers! The effect of daggers is guaranteed. Remember that.'

Suddenly they heard the voice of Haj Abdullah. 'Won't do this, won't do that,' he bellowed. 'Well, off you go, lads, off to your studies! Go on, go home, no more nonsense!'

The boys exchanged glances, but slowly they got up and left, pursing their lips.

Adil climbed the stairs to Abu Sabir's house. Um Sabir was just then coming down, holding a child by the hand. She raised her black veil. 'How nice to see you, Adil,' she said. 'Please go on in. Abu Sabir's upstairs waiting for you. I'm off to do some shopping, but I'll be back soon and we'll have coffee.'

Abu Sabir, still in his pyjamas, greeted him warmly: 'Welcome! Welcome, Adil! Good morning! How are you? How's the job going?'

Adil sat down in a chair with a rush seat, took a cucumber from the table and began to munch it. They went over the latest developments in Abu Sabir's compensation case. Adil had convinced Abu Sabir that he should request compensation for his injuries and subsequent unemployment in accordance with local and Israeli regulations. After several letters to the mayor and to the military governor of the West Bank and Gaza, Abu Sabir had been granted an interview with the military governor of Nablus. The governor had informed him that he was responsible only for matters relating to national security and the preservation of order and hence had no jurisdiction in the case. But he had written a letter of recommendation to the director of social services in Nazareth, who had duly replied to the military governor. The latter, after receiving this reply, had written another letter to the director of social services. This had led to a second reply from the director to Abu Sabir, in which he stated that it was not possible for the social services to provide assistance. On hearing this news, the military governor had advised Abu Sabir to hire a lawyer and file a suit against the civil authorities.

'But what can I do, Adil?' complained Abu Sabir. 'The cost of all this travel back and forth is eating up everything I own, just like the way my fingers went. I've already sold one of my wife's bracelets and all I got out of it was a lot of coming and going and exhaustion. I've had it, Adil. Sabir will just have to leave school and go to work. That's our fate and we must accept it. What's written on your forehead must be seen by your eyes. When your enemy's also your judge, who can you turn to?'

'No, Abu Sabir, don't say that. That's no way to talk! Are you going to give up your rights without a fight? Is that what we agreed on? Look at Mahmoud, he kept at it and he won in the end. You have to keep going too until you get what you have a right to. And Sabir must stay at school until everything's settled.'

Tears came to Abu Sabir's eyes. He gripped Adil by the hand: 'By God, Adil, I don't know how I'll ever repay your kindness. Your standing by me through this ordeal means the world to me. But I'm not sure what to do. The whole country's in turmoil, the Jews couldn't care less about people like me. What will I gain from this constant travelling around?'

'Come on, Abu Sabir! Your rights won't be delivered to you while you sit comfortably at home. You have to keep at it, make a determined effort. It's not just a matter between Arabs and Israelis. It's a question of workers and employers. And if you can't find a way to fight for your rights on this issue, how will you learn to fight for them in other areas? You must keep at it. You'll have to hire a lawyer.'

Abu Sabir allowed himself to be persuaded, and the two men discussed in detail how to go about things. 'But,' he murmured, 'my wife won't agree to sell any more bracelets unless it's for food. She doesn't believe I'll ever get compensation from the Jews. She says they stole our country lock, stock and barrel, so why shouldn't they steal my compensation money too? What do you think?'

Adil smiled and shook his head, well aware that these were Abu Sabir's own doubts, not those of his wife. But he merely said, 'Even if it's as she says, it's up to you not to give in easily. You've got to give those people a real headache by pushing on, forcing them to compensate you for the injury and loss you've suffered. Come on, friend, give them a hard time, that's the least you can do.' Adil paused, and then went on. 'In any case, some workers have gained their rights by persisting. They've received excellent compensation. The company's obliged to compensate a worker, whether he's got an official work permit or not. So why not try like they have?'

'I understand,' said Abu Sabir, nodding. 'But my wife's stubborn; she only understands cooking and children. I overheard her whispering to Sabir last night, trying to persuade him to leave school. And the poor kid agreed. I pretended to be asleep. But let's drop the subject. She might come in any minute and hear us.'

Seeing the smile on Adil's face, Abu Sabir defended himself by saying, 'Don't smile. You'll soon get married, and then you'll understand the meaning of responsibility.'

Marry? thought Adil. Me? How could I? And when? With nine mouths and the kidney machine to support? And who on earth would want to marry a labourer like me? A factory girl at best. And for the most part they're uneducated, capable only of cooking, cleaning and breeding. Yet even they've developed bourgeois aspirations. These days, social class has become an essential factor in marriage too.

Disgustedly, Adil knocked the ash off his cigarette and

rose to leave.

'I'm off, Abu Sabir. See you tomorrow.'

'Leaving without having coffee! That's absolutely impossible, there's no way you're leaving without coffee. I'll make it myself. I've learned how to use my other hand. Please sit down. It's still early. Today's Saturday and the town's filled with Arabs and Jews. Where are you off to anyway?'

Abu Sabir was back in a few moments, carrying two cups of coffee.

'Hey, I forgot to tell you the latest news about Zuhdi,' he said, smiling.

'Zuhdi? What about him?' Adil asked eagerly. 'Has Saadiyya been to see him?'

Handing Adil his cup of coffee, Abu Sabir stared out of the window again. 'The wife's late,' he commented. He sat down on the edge of the bed, sipping his coffee, and explained: 'Zuhdi's turned intellectual! You know what he asked for? Books!'

'Books!'

'Yes, by God. He hasn't asked for food, cigarettes or clothes – just books. Can you believe it?'

'What kind of books?'

'Ones I've never heard of before. Saadiyya's learned their titles by heart. She wants you to drop by and talk about these books. What's interesting is that they aren't just stories, but serious studies. Ha, ha, ha! Imagine Zuhdi reading stuff like that! Who'd have believed it! Glory be to God who changes all but never changes Himself. Zuhdi reading books! That's rich, eh, Adil? But hang on: maybe he just wanted them for his friends in prison.'

'And maybe for himself. The prisoners use their time very well, I'm told. If I weren't worried about you, Abu Sabir, I'd wish you six months in prison, so you'd become serious like them.'

Abu Sabir looked at him reproachfully and pointed to his bookcase with its broken glass door. A few tattered books lay on one shelf. 'Have you forgotten that I'm a great reader, Adil?'

He went and picked out a fat book which he handed to Adil.

'You know *Les Misérables*? Finest book ever written. How would Zuhdi ever read this? This is a book that needs the persistence of an Abu Sabir, and a mind like his too. I don't think the books Zuhdi's asked for are as good as this one. Look.'

He began leafing through the book admiringly. Then he stared anxiously out of the window.

'The wife's late,' he said. 'She must be gossiping at Um Badawi's window. I'll have to cure her of that. The woman abandons me for hours on end and doesn't worry about me at all. When I ask her why, she goes on and on about all her hard work and responsbilities. When she gets back, I'll take another one of her bracelets, even if she fills the whole house with screams and curses!'

Adil smiled and took another cucumber from the table.

Um Sabir slapped her son's hand stretched out to the box of medlars. 'Leave them alone! It's not our fruit.'

'Please, Um Sabir,' the greengrocer said sympathetically, 'let him take one. And give thanks to God!'

He handed several to the boy, while his mother protested in embarrassment: 'But medlars are expensive, Abu Hamdi.'

'Nice people like you deserve them,' he replied expansively. 'Nothing's too expensive for nice people. Eat up, son. Before the occupation, medlars were food for sparrows. Now they're only for the rich and pampered. They cost forty-five qurush a pound! What a rotten life! Eat up, boy, eat up. God damn the occupation and bring it to an end!'

Um Sabir, overcome by the man's generosity, poured out a stream of praises and blessings upon him. Then she pulled the child to one side and raised her finger in warning: 'If you tell your brothers, I'll kill you!'

The boy didn't answer but went on devouring the fruit, the juice pouring down his chin. An Israeli army officer approached the stand. 'How much are the *tappouzim*?' he asked, using the Hebrew word for oranges.

The greengrocer rubbed his hands, smiling: 'Whatever you like, *Adon*. Just one price, as there's just one God. Thirteen a pound. These naval oranges are like gold.'

The officer made a face and turned back to his young wife

standing behind him. He spoke to her in Hebrew and she shook her head, but their little blonde daughter pointed at the medlars and muttered something.

Um Sabir stood staring at the family through her veil, filled with anger and envy. I hope they choke on them, she thought. I hope the fruit's poisonous and kills all three of them! My kids would give anything for a medlar or two, but these people gorge on them like wild beasts. God destroy this nation of Muhammad for letting these vile people come and go as they like in our country and our towns! May seventy evil eyes get these enemies of ours!

She pulled at her son. 'Come on, Muhammad. We're going home now.'

The little boy stamped his foot and pointed at a bunch of bananas, but Um Sabir tugged him away, still keeping an eye on the Israeli woman. She, in turn, was looking at Muhammad with genuine concern, but her stare sent Um Sabir into a rage. She slapped the child hard on the back of his head and he cried out. The Israeli woman put out her arm to shield the boy from his mother's blows. 'No, no! That's not nice,' she said in Arabic. 'Not nice.'

Um Sabir adjusted her veil, the veins in her neck were pulsing in fury. What's my son got to do with you, you slut? Sorry for him, are you? If you're so full of compassion, why don't you ask your husband about my husband's lost fingers?

She stared angrily at the stars on the officer's epaulettes. How many men have you killed, you bastard? How many prisoners have you castrated? Smile, will you! My, what a fine polite man you are! What, pay cash for your fruit, do you? How terribly nice of you and Moshe Dayan! Our whole country's yours, and all it produces is yours, so why bother to pay? Laughing at us, eh? Well, the whole world does that too, so why shouldn't you?

The smile faded from the man's face when he saw the anger and resentment in Um Sabir's eyes, and he muttered something in Hebrew to his wife. She turned away from

157

the boy and his mother and busied herself selecting some fresh medlars.

Suddenly, seemingly out of nowhere, a young man, his face shrouded in a white *kufiyya*, sprang at the officer. His raised hand came down with lightning speed, and a dagger sank to the hilt in the nape of the officer's neck. He let out a deep groan and slumped over the box of medlars, his blood spurting out as though from a fountain. His wife screamed and then just stood there, terror-stricken and dazed. The little girl covered her face, and her blonde hair tumbled down over her forehead and hands. Um Sabir gripped her son's hand tight and retreated a few steps, yelling, 'You're a hero, you've done well!'

The young man turned and stared into her face for a moment, then through the *kufiyya* that muffled his face, said, 'Better go home right away.'

She knew that voice! She recognized those eyes! Who are you? Who are you? I know you, I've seen you before, but where?

The young man took to his heels and no one stopped him. Um Sabir still stood close to the wall, breathing heavily and burying her son's head in her skirts. The greengrocer was beating his head and shouting, 'Oh God, I'm ruined, utterly ruined!'

The officer still lay across the box of fruit, barely breathing, while people nearby stared in grim silence. Then suddenly they began to run, jostling one another in their panic. The street was soon filled with people running while the officer's wife screamed and pointed at the muffled young man who was disappearing into the crowd. 'Get him! Stop him!' But no one did.

The little girl now took her hands from her eyes and saw her father lying there, crumpled up over the box of fruit, the dagger still buried in his neck. Too shocked to speak, she stretched out a hand towards him. Then she began banging her head wildly against the metal support of the shop awning, and finally collapsed on the ground.

Um Sabir's eyes met those of the Israeli woman; she seemed to be both begging for help and screaming in pain. Involuntarily, something was shaking the locked doors of Um Sabir's heart. She softened and responded to the woman's unspoken plea. 'God have mercy on you!' she muttered.

Muhammad, clutching his mother's legs, was staring from the dead man, to his widow, to the little girl. He began to cry. And the sight of the little girl, lying there on the pavement with her legs exposed up to the crotch, made Um Sabir think of her own girls, of all little girls. She took off her veil and covered the girl's naked thighs, murmuring as she bent over the unconscious child, 'I'm so sorry for you, my daughter.' This made her son grip her all the tighter and his crying grew louder.

There were still people hurrying about, locking the doors of shops and racing down the alleyways, looking for dark corners to hide in. Abu Hamdi, the greengrocer, stood in the middle of the street, shouting for help, but none came.

Muhammad gave one last tug at his mother's skirts, and raced off into the crowd. Um Sabir called to him, glancing back all the while at the little girl lying unconscious in the street. Then she forced herself to move and caught up with her son, grabbing him by the coat while he yelled and squirmed. Then she came back and extended a hand to the widow who was moaning to herself in Hebrew. Gently touching her shoulder, she said, 'God help you, sister. May God help you . . .'

A strong hand tugged at her from behind. 'Go home, Um Sabir,' said a voice.

She turned towards the man; it was Adil, standing right behind her. Her voice choking, she whispered, 'Oh, Adil . . .' He propelled her away saying, 'Go home to your children! Go home!'

After a final pat on the Israeli woman's shoulder, she turned and hurried away through the mass of running people.

Adil spoke to the Israeli woman. She rested her head on Adil's shoulder, moaning to herself.

'Calm yourself,' he said gently in Hebrew. He splashed water on the little girl's face, who stirred.

A man rushed past, yelling, 'Leave them alone, Adil. The patrol cars are coming.'

He ignored the warning, moved over towards the body and took the man's wrist to examine his pulse. Another passer-by tugged at his shoulder. 'Leave the pig alone!' he cried. 'There's a patrol on its way. Can't you see the stars of the man's rank?'

Adil tore the stars off and tossed them to the ground. Then he picked up the little girl, hoisted her onto his shoulders, and walked off down the empty street. Her mother followed behind, silently weeping.

Usama hid in a dark corner of the street. He unwound the *kufiyya* from his head and threw it to the ground. Looking carefully left and right, he moved off into the crowd. He felt eyes devouring his face and imaginary fingers pointing at his hand, which felt as though he were still gripping a dagger. He ran on to the end of the street. The patrol cars were coming. He climbed the steps to his uncle's house. Basil was waiting. Without saying a word, they ran across the open courtyard and down a passage behind the marble pillars. Basil moved a stone in the wall, and a secret door opened that led into an ancient vault.

Basil lit a small flashlight and went down the crumbling steps. Usama followed him.

'Did anyone recognize you?' Basil asked.

Usama drew a deep breath. A pungent odour of decay was all about him. Crates of explosives lay along one side of the vault. He felt their cold wood. 'I'm not sure,' he answered. 'Saafan may have been there.'

Basil turned abruptly and shone the flashlight in his cousin's face. 'Saafan? That's a disaster! Are you sure?'

'No, I'm not. Come on, let's get moving. We have to hide quickly. We can't take risks. It was probably Saafan. And he must have recognized me. I saw him in the shop once. What's more important is that some of our men are waiting over there. You know what you're supposed to do?'

'Trust God and me,' said Basil. 'Hani and I will distribute

161

what's necessary. And I know the password.'

Usama took him by the shoulders.

'Be careful, Basil,' he warned. 'This is a serious business. You know the consequences. I won't repeat the advice I gave you earlier. But don't make any decisions without consulting Lina. That's crucial. She's a very solid girl. And she's had lots of experience. Now, let me kiss you goodbye. I may not see you again. Be a man, Basil. Don't trust anyone. Especially the people in this house.'

They moved off down the long, cold vault. At the end Basil opened a piece of the wall from the inside and Usama found himself in the ablutions area of the Great Mosque. He emerged along with the worshippers and hired a taxi to take him to a village. Soon he could no longer see the city behind him.

He walked for an hour without stopping, clambering along rough mountain paths, then finally sat down on the edge of a rock. He took off his shoes and sweater, and opened the neck of his shirt.

The sun was setting. The May breezes moved through the cypress and olive groves. He stretched out on the grass, resting his head on a smooth rock. He felt lost, wanted to break down and weep. His eyes swam up into the blue space above him. Shadows of oak trees. The olive trees and umbrella pines that grew deep in the mountains. Grape vines on the slopes.

He raised his hand and stared at it. The same hand that had written poetry about love and peace. And about the sacrificial lamb!

He watched the play of light on the veins of his hand. Amazement. Confusion. He was sensitive and confused, like many other men. He touched the earth he loved. Yes, but. The time for poetry and dreams of passion was past. And this hand. This very hand! Those two other hands that had covered the shocked face of a little blonde girl. The mother had screamed 'Get him!' An unseen hand seemed to grip his heart. Loneliness, isolation, silence. Far away a peasant played his flute while another sang:

> Mountain, greet the plain and the valley.
> Greet the trees that line the flanks of my country.
> Though the enemy harvests our fields,
> I will seed the ground again with my sons.

A mist of poetry seemed to hover above his head. Why are we so moved by songs of loss? Are we a nation of romantics? Well, not any more. Love lying broken at your feet makes your soul a commodity in the market of blood. But I'm here. On this earth, in spite of everything. I'm here. And I'll stay here. Let the leader push me onto the dirtiest plane in any Arab airport and let fire-spitting engines bear me to Lisbon or America or the oil states. Let any force on this earth transport me wherever its mood decides, to any spot as yet unknown in time and space. I'm here. I've returned. To this rock. To this hollow. And this hand, stained with blood, is still a bridge of freedom over a river of pain. Now I raise it, now I let it drop, it's an eagle's wing, swift enough to cut the sound barrier with its edge. My voice thunders; the Katyushas and the napalm roar. May the earth shake when I walk. May unheeding eyes watch me if I sleep. I'm moving towards the light along the dark paths of anger.

He laced up his shoes and walked away, whistling cheerfully.

The violent knocking rattled the decrepit front door in its frame. The woman sat up in bed and muttered a string of silent prayers before putting her feet on the floor. The knocking started again, and she felt her blood pressure begin to rise and her weak heart almost stop.

God protect me, she said to herself. Let it be good news, not bad. If the bridge were open at night, it could even be Usama.

'Open the door. Open up!' a voice bellowed from outside the door.

The Jews! Have mercy, oh Lord! What could they want?

She put on the light, hurried across the room, and opened the door. A group of soldiers burst into the room.

'Is Usama al-Karmi here?' yelled one.

She felt for the wall to avoid collapsing. Her eyes stared, her heart was pounding, she couldn't speak.

The soldiers split off into the four rooms; they drew their guns as they searched for the fugitive. Wardrobe doors crashed and banged. The old woman cried out, hoarse but unheard: 'Usama? Usama?'

A soldier stood directly in front of her. 'Where's Usama?' he demanded.

'Usama? He's in Amman. He's not here.'

'Where's Usama?'

She dropped her hand from the wall and stared straight into the soldier's face. He seized her hand and pulled her towards the wardrobe. 'Whose are these clothes?'

'They belong to my son Usama.'

'And where's Usama?'

'He's gone to Amman.'

'He hasn't gone to Amman. He's hiding somewhere here.'

He left her standing near the wardrobe and began searching under the bed, under the table, behind the curtains. He opened drawers, looked through papers, scattered books.

'Your son's very interested in the affairs of factory workers. Why is that?'

She sat trembling on the edge of the bed. The soldier was reading through newspaper clippings. 'Your son collects items about the workers. Why is that?'

'My son Usama, may God bless him, is well educated and interested in everything.'

'Your son Usama, may God bless him, is interested in matters concerning the workers. What's his connection with them?'

His sarcastic tone silenced her. He raised his eyes demanding a response, but her only reply was a long, silent stare of disgust. The soldier moderated his tone. 'Where was your son,' he asked, 'when the loudspeakers toured the town asking all the men to gather at the Salahiyya School?'

'You mean,' she replied slowly, 'you mean the day of the assassination of the . . .'

'Yes, the day of the officer's assassination. Where was your son?'

She stared down at the tips of her slippers and realized that she had only her nightdress on. Oh God! She stood up quickly, ashamed of her appearance.

'Stay where you are,' shouted the soldier, raising his weapon.

She gazed coolly at the machine-gun. 'Put that thing away, please,' she said, 'and stop your silly games. I want to put my dressing gown on.'

She reached out to the machine-gun, pushed it out of her way and walked over to the wardrobe. He kept close behind her, his gun still at the ready. 'You seem to have been expecting our visit!'

She didn't answer, but put on her dressing gown and covered her hair with her prayer scarf.

'Well, weren't you expecting us to come?'

'No,' she replied coldly.

'And yet you're not afraid!'

Afraid? Why should I be afraid? There isn't much life left before me anyway. And the only person I'm afraid for is in danger right now. Should I fear for my own old age and not for his youth?

'You act as though you're used to our presence in your home!' said the soldier.

I'm used to your presence in my neighbours' homes. The only time I leave my windows is to go to sleep.

She picked up her prayer beads and sat down once more on the edge of the bed. She began telling her beads. Raising her eyes she saw him staring down at her angrily.

You're not a likeable man, by God, she reflected. If I weren't so afraid for my son, I'd pray God to make your mother grieve for you! May God forgive me for that! But nothing will happen to you except what God has decreed. There is no God but He, the Living, the Everlasting; no drowsiness overcomes Him, neither does He sleep. To Him belongs dominion over heaven and earth . . .*

'I asked you a question,' he persisted.

'What do you want?'

'Madam, you're acting as though you expected our visit.'

'And who doesn't expect your visit these days? We're under occupation. What else should we expect?'

'Were you expecting our visit?'

* The phrase is from the Koran, Sura 2, verse 256.

166

She smiled, but didn't answer. She began mumbling a prayer.

He yelled at her: 'I asked you a question, madam!'

Her heart pounded. She blinked hard, then stared at him. 'So what do you want?' she asked. 'This is my home. You're here; search all you want. Usama's in Amman. If you want him, you must follow him there.'

He shook his head and muttered something. Then he commented, 'We *will* follow him to Amman. Do you think it would be difficult?'

She smiled. 'Why are you smiling?' he asked softly.

She shook her beads and went on mumbling her prayers, but did not reply. The soldier turned away and began gathering armfuls of clothes from the wardrobe and throwing them on the floor. All her clothes, Usama's clothes, their shoes, a bag of worn-out socks. He opened the bag and pulled out the socks, one by one. He opened a plastic bag filled with dried apricot paste, peered inside and sniffed at it. 'What's this?'

'Dried apricot paste.'

'Ah, dried apricot paste, eh? Do you fast during Ramadan?'

Yes, I do indeed fast during Ramadan and I perform the five daily prayers and I pray to God to take you all away and relieve us of the sight of you.

The clothes were now piled in a heap on the floor, books and papers scattered all over the place. More soldiers came in; they consulted with each other in Hebrew, shaking their heads.

She stood up and looked out of the window; neighbours peered out of the lighted windows nearby. Um Sadiq was hiding behind a curtain but could still be glimpsed observing the scene through a narrow gap in the Venetian blinds. She smiled encouragingly and Usama's mother nodded in reply and murmured verses from the Koran to herself: 'Did we not send flocks of birds to fling against them stones of baked clay, thus rendering them like chaff digested?'

The soldiers had paused to confer with one another. Then all except one left the room. He picked up the papers the other soldier had questioned her about. Then he sat down on an office chair. 'Where's your son?' he asked politely.

A sense of fatigue, even boredom, came over her. 'What do you want with my son?'

'Nothing. Just a few minutes of his time, then we'll return him safely to you.'

May God never grant you peace, you bastard of accursed parents, taking advantage of my advanced age.

'My son, God bless him, left for Amman three days ago and hasn't come back yet.'

'When will he be back?'

'In a week or two maybe. I don't know.'

'When did he leave the house?'

'I told you, three days ago.'

'When did you last see him?'

She thought for a moment. 'He ate his breakfast, then left.'

'Did he take any clothes with him?'

She remembered that he had not and trembled at the thought, but then controlled herself. 'Yes, he did.'

'What did he take?'

Don't tear my soul to pieces! May God poison your body now, this very evening!

'He took a suit and a change of underwear.'

He asked another question that she didn't hear. She was thinking about this business of the clothes, which hadn't occurred to her before. Her head throbbed from her rising blood pressure. Her chest felt tight; sweat broke out on her forehead.

'Madam, I asked you a question, but you didn't reply.'

She stood up, tried to reach her medicine but tottered and fell back on the edge of the bed, nearly fainting.

'Are you ill?' the soldier asked, his voice suddenly full of concern.

My complaint is to God about you, you criminals. You'll

take my son away! Where did he go? Not to Amman. Did you do it, Usama? Did you lie to your mother, apple of my eye? Oh, Usama what did you do? Where did you go? They say the officer was killed by a young man whose head was covered in a white *kufiyya*. Your father's *kufiyya*, Usama. No, no, it doesn't make sense. Usama wouldn't hurt a fly. Usama's compassionate, kind-hearted, meek as a lamb. Yes, I still remember that lamb we sacrificed for the feast, and that funny poem Usama wrote. No. It can't be. My son Usama's looking for a job, and as soon as he finds one he's going to marry his cousin Nuwar, the fairest flower of her family. A girl with lovely straight hair, and skin as pure and smooth as milk. Yes, may the Prophet be praised! I should relax. I've nothing to worry about. But it's impossible. I can't. There's no relief, no peace, no way to rid myself of this pressure.

She breathed in short gasps as she wiped the sweat from her forehead with the edge of her veil. I pray to God to forgive my sins, I turn to Him in repentance. God save you, Usama, you, the dearest thing in the world to me. God bless you and keep you safe, Usama, in every step you take. God willing, you'll return, protected and watched over by God's angels.

'Are you feeling ill, madam?'

The prayer beads dropped from her hand; she swayed and grasped the edge of the bed for support.

The soldier came closer. 'Have you got some medicine you can take?' he asked. 'Can I help you?'

Panting, she cried, 'Open the window and call for Um Sadiq.'

The soldier did as she asked, but Um Sadiq, frightened, disappeared behind the curtains.

'Um Sadiq!' the solder called out again.

There was still no response, so he shouted angrily, 'Um Sadiq, come and see to your neighbour!'

He then left the room, casting anxious glances at Usama's mother as he went. What if she died? The word would spread all over town that Israeli soldiers had killed a poor woman in her seventies for no reason. There would be the usual rumours, protests, petitions from the mayor and the Red Cross. Israel's peace-loving image would be distorted and attacked. The woman was not worth the risk of such ridicule, he decided.

He ran down the stairs, shouting out an order. The soldiers climbed into their vehicles and drove off; light still streamed from every window in the neighbourhood.

Um Sadiq came in, breathing hard. 'Thank God you're all right, my dear!' she said. 'Where's your medicine?'

Um Usama pointed to the table. Her neighbour rifled through the sheets of paper and newspaper clippings until she found a glass bottle. She handed a capsule to Um Usama.

'Here, take this, my dear,' she said. 'Drink up and may it give you comfort and good health. May God rid us of the sight of them. Oh, how my heart went out to you as soon as they entered your home. I longed to be right here at your side, but there wasn't much I could do, as you very well know. But I saw everything that went on. The first soldier, the one with the moustache, God damn him, I saw how he pointed his machine-gun at you and my heart stopped. I said to myself, "Um Usama, you're as good as dead." God damn them all! May God blacken their fate! Come on, Um Usama, just sleep now. I'll stay with you till morning. Don't worry now, that's what friends are for, my dear. This is a difficult moment, but it will pass.'

Um Usama burst into a flood of hot tears. My son! My boy! Where are you now, my precious son? Could you really have done it, Usama? How could an angel, a prince, the son of a prince, do such a thing? It doesn't make sense, there's no sense in it.

Her neighbour tried to comfort her. 'Don't get so upset, Um Usama,' she urged. 'Don't worry, it's a difficult moment, but it will pass.'

She too shed tears in genuine sympathy for her friend

and for Usama. She was sure they'd find him, wherever he might be, and skin him alive. She assumed that he'd been recognized; the place was thick with spies. She grieved at the thought of how little chance Um Usama had had to enjoy her son and his youth, to rejoice at seeing him married.

Um Usama cried out faintly.

'What is it, Um Usama? Just tell me what you want, dear.'

Um Usama sighed. 'Can you look in the top drawer for the white *kufiyya* that belonged to my husband?' she asked. 'Please give it to me, Um Sadiq, let me smell my dead husband's fragrance in it. It will bless and comfort me.'

Her friend opened the drawer, but it was empty. She searched through the piles of clothing on the floor, but there was no sign of the white *kufiyya*. Um Usama's eyes followed her every movement and finally she shook her head in despair and began to weep again. You did do it, Usama! You did it, may God forgive you!

She opened her eyes. She felt a prick in her arm and saw a doctor beside her; Adil was standing at his side, whispering to him. The doctor left, but Adil sat on the edge of her bed and kissed her hand. 'Auntie,' he said, 'I hope you're feeling better.'

She gripped his hand tightly, and the tears flowed. 'Usama did it, Adil; he did it!'

Adil bowed his head without answering. She continued to sob. 'I've had no chance to enjoy him, Adil,' she cried. 'I wanted to marry him to Nuwar, but now he's done this, and broken my heart.'

Sombre images filled Adil's mind. The dead officer, his grieving widow, the little girl stretched out on the ground, her pale, bare legs partly covered by Um Sabir's veil. People running through the streets, someone yelling, 'Leave the pig alone!' Bitterness flooded his heart. My cousin kills a man and I carry off his daughter. Tragedy or farce? Still, the memory of the Israeli woman's head on his shoulder, despite all the boundaries that divided people, seemed to open the horizons of this narrow world.

A world of freedom and people. Streets pulsing with life and movement. Trees heavy with the blossoms of May. The smell of warm grass and the glint of the sun on everything. Emotion surged up in him and he skipped a few steps along the empty pavement. He got into a taxi and listened to a cheerful song on the radio; his heart throbbed with joy. His wife Saadiyya, his children, Adil al-Karmi and Abu Sabir came to his mind. Nablus! God bless you. I've almost died of longing for you, Nablus! Zuhdi was free.

He got out of the taxi in the main square and was greeted on the pavements and in the shops and alleys by storms of good wishes and kisses.

'A thousand praises to God for your safety, Zuhdi.'

'Come and have some *kinafa* to celebrate your release.'

'Come on in, friend, don't hurry home to your family. By tomorrow you'll be sick of your wife's voice and the children's noise. Sit down for a while.'

Sick of them? How could he possibly be sick of them? No more cups of tea with television screens in them, no more faces watching him morning, noon and night, at breakfast and at supper.

He quickened his pace. When he reached his own neighbourhood the meat and vegetable sellers let out screams of surprise and delight and shouted upstairs to his wife; but she, oblivious to the outside world, was busy having her weekly bath. The steam and noise of the primus stove filled

173

the small bathroom.

Zuhdi bounded up the stairs, his heart pounding. He pushed open the door with his foot and it creaked loudly. Ammar, his little boy, was sitting on the floor playing with some saucepan lids. He stared up in amazement at his father's face. 'Daddy!' he screamed. 'It's you! You're back!'

Zuhdi silenced him with a kiss. Saadiyya opened the bathroom door a little and called, 'Who is it?'

He pushed open the door and pulled her warm, damp body to him. Saadiyya began to weep, gazing at her husband's face through the clouds of steam; a sudden terror showed on her face, red with emotion and the heat of the bath. 'Zuhdi, you didn't escape, did you?'

'No, no, not at all. They let me out. Don't talk . . .'

He kissed her warm flesh all over and buried his nose in the combined perfume of soap and woman. Let me forget. Help me forget. I've dreamed so much, so very much, but I never imagined a reception as lavish, as generous, as this. These breasts, these thighs, havens of safety in an occupied land. The human race breeds on despite all disasters, that's the people's one remaining pleasure. This treasure is my fortress that no intruder can violate. The fertile land receives the seed and turns it into a profusion of production and consumption. But if the producer leaves his post, little mouths grow hungry and bracelets fall from plump arms.

Where are your bracelets, Saadiyya? All gone? I'll buy you some more. And the children will eat well. Tomorrow I'll go west to look for work. They still need our hands over there, and that way they're sure of our silence. But I've learned to be clever in silence and clever in speech. And when I talk, you'll listen; you won't budge, and so you'll help me to forget, to forget everything that's happened. I've dreamed so much, so very much. Oh, Saadiyya! Why can't the world leave me alone? Food, a bed, and this . . . That's all a good man like me wants. And you're good too, Saadiyya! How good you are!

He sat on the bed, surrounded by his children. Hamada! How've you been, young man? How long it's been, Hamada! How've they been treating you, son? They hit you? Don't worry. Fighting strengthens weak muscles and fires up the brain. And what's school done to that brain of yours? Where've you got to in history now? Have you learned about the French revolution yet? Well, I've studied too, son. I've studied a lot and heard even more. I've seen a child, a little boy of five, break through prison walls and make grown men shed tears of pain and anger. Even the soldiers cried. They remembered their own sons and wept. I read Abu Salim's letters aloud to him and heard the news of Masouda and her white calf. The calf died but Masouda lived, feeding other cow's calves with milk from her swollen udders. Don't despair, my boy; history moves on – everything depends on the way you react to things.

'What have you got to eat, Saadiyya? So these days even lentils have become "aristocratic"? Why? How much are they? Never mind. Hamada, run down to the grocer's and get some food on credit; tell him I'll settle my account in a few days. Tomorrow I'm going west to look for a job.'

He stood behind his wife in the dark kitchen, watching her prepare the meal. Poor dear. Even her smile couldn't hide her drawn and haggard expression – worry and the difficult times she'd been through were written all over her face. And what about this swarm of locusts, this batch of tireless children who never stop eating? All praise to the Creator! Why is it that children pour down like rain on poor people like us and take over our whole lives, when nothing like that ever happens to the rich? Is that God's wisdom? What wisdom? Is it wise for the majority to be so numerous and empty-bellied while the elite remain a stuffed-bellied minority? I learned a lot from those prison sessions with the Adil there, and I'll learn even more from Adil al-Karmi.

'Well, look who's here! It's Adil al-Karmi! Let me give you a hug, brother! God bless you and all those you love! Please sit down; here, let's go into the other room. How are

175

you, my friend? It's been a long time. Hey, Adil, if only you knew what I've been through. I'll tell you everything. And thank you for the books you sent. I really appreciate all you've done; I hope I can pay you back when times are better. Will you have some tea? Please, I insist. No, impossible; you simply must have something to drink.'

Zuhdi turned to his son. 'Hamada, bring some tea, son!' he called. 'Some nice spiced tea. You know how we used to make tea in prison? We'd tear up an egg box and put it under a tin hanging from a broomstick between two buckets. And it was superb tea, especially when it gave us TV serials in the reflections such as you'd never imagine. Yes, we saw Izdihar in them, and Nidal, and there was Um Salim's oven, and chicken and onions and thyme, and poor Masouda with her dead calf. My God make things easy for my comrades still in prison. Oh yes, they were real comrades. They thought I was a spy when I went in, but by the time I left, I was a comrade. I got educated, not only school subjects but special evening sessions too. Proletariat, capitalism, bourgeoisie, compradorism, and all that. Led by another Adil. The Adil in that prison's a scary fellow though. He's got a sharp mind and a hand that can split a head open without using a wrench. Yes, I'll tell you everything sooner or later. But what's your news? What about Abu Sabir?'

Adil poured the spiced tea without smiling. 'Tomorrow morning Abu Sabir and I are going to Haifa to see the lawyer,' he said. 'It's a pity you and I won't be able to go to work together. I'd like to see how everybody welcomes you back. Anyway, it doesn't matter. The important thing is that the court's decided in Abu Sabir's favour. The lower court in Nablus awarded him eighty-four thousand Israeli pounds compensation.'

'That's great! He can open his own shop and live in comfort.'

Adil sighed audibly.

'What's wrong, Adil my friend?' asked Zuhdi anxiously.

'Nothing wrong, is there? You're not sad he's going to get compensation? Don't be like those clever types. Hungry people can't afford to be angry.'

'No, no,' replied Adil. 'That's not what I'm worried about. But the company claims it's bankrupt and can't pay. And it seems we're going to have to face some harsh new regulations.'

'What's happened so far?'

'Abu Sabir hasn't received any compensation.'

'Come on, you don't mean it!'

'Really, that's the way it is. The Haifa court sent Abu Sabir a copy of the so-called bankruptcy affidavit as though that were the end of the matter.'

'And what have you done about it?'

'So far nothing. But I've persuaded Abu Sabir to push ahead and not stop now; that's why we're going to Haifa tomorrow to see the lawyer. In cases like these, as I understand it, the law usually provides for the appointment of a committee to establish proof of bankruptcy.'

He thought for a moment. 'But you know what hurts the most, Zuhdi?' he asked. 'The look on his wife's face. It's as though she's blaming me for all the effort and expense that they've wasted on a cause that she thought was lost from the start.'

'Come on, my friend,' said Zuhdi encouragingly. 'Don't despair.'

'But I *do* despair,' Adil murmured. 'I fight my despair with despair itself. Do you understand? Well, neither do I. I don't really understand this strange mixture of feelings I have, I don't know how to explain what's going through my mind. I'm confused and I can't exactly define my own position. Peace, brotherhood – hopes of idiots and dreams of birds. Maybe. I don't know. Yet I still dream. I dream of the impossible. But I ask you, is it possible to grow roses from thorns?'

'The thorns aren't there to produce roses,' Zuhdi answered, 'they're there to protect them.'

'Well, I still dream,' Adil answered.
'God's peace be with you, then,' said Zuhdi quietly.
'And with all the world,' returned Adil.

The smell of baking bread and burning dung filled the air. Cool evening breezes rustled the branches of the plum tree. Beneath the towering walnut, men sat round a fire boiling a pot of sage tea. They were listening to the news on a transistor radio. The American Secretary of Defence had made a new statement about arms shipments to Israel. Phantom jets. More and more Phantoms. Billions of dollars flooding into Israel's treasury. The old men muttered grim prayers, praising God and invoking blessings on the people of the Prophet Muhammad. The young men cursed and blasphemed . . . Arab oil revenue turned into Phantoms! So much for Arab unity!

As if to forget their wounds they asked Usama to tell his story once more. Yes, the dagger sank into his neck like a spoon into yoghurt. I ran along the street without anyone stopping me. People were gloating. There was a feeling of triumph, great triumph. One woman shouted, 'You're a hero; well done!' To encourage crime doesn't indicate a very humane soul, it's true. But what remains in this breast? Only bitterness and knots of anger.

The flames flickered on the peasants' faces. Abu al-Raad thundered, 'This land's yours. Take it back with United Nations resolutions. Take it back with poetry and songs of return. Kneel in prayer to God a million times. God gives victory only to those who seize it.'

Cool breezes, the smell of the oven fire and burning

dung. In the distance a reed flute serenaded the wheat, now ready for harvesting. Usama's eyes filled with tears of longing. The heart always tends towards waywardness and madness, he told himself, and that flute reminds you of weddings yet to come. Hands clasped in readiness for the dance, brightly coloured scarves floating, feet tapping the ground and sending the spirit soaring, high as the seventh heaven. But a plane takes off from an Arab airport bound for Lisbon; a government flings you from one airport to another. Other countries spit you out, and your own land receives you at last. This land, this much-worshipped land! Youthful ardour, and young hearts burning with passion! Season of love wasted in exile and songs of yearning!

Abu al-Raad thundered on: 'Don't talk of "humanity", of "love". Love's dead, friends. You must arm yourselves with wolves' fangs. Stop being meek lambs ready only for tyrants to skin.'

The flames danced over the faces of the men. They'd drunk strong sage tea. Gradually the fire waned and the old men left the young ones and retired. Abu al-Raad drew a primitive map on the ground beneath the walnut tree. 'At dawn we'll be here, waiting for the buses carrying the workers. Don't shoot to kill at the people in the buses. Just scare them, that's all.'

The men walked along the mountain paths they knew as well as they knew the paths of their own lives. Night. Stars but no moon. Silence broken only by the croaking of frogs. Cicadas pulsing in the branches of the plum and olive trees. Rubber-soled shoes. Civilian dress. Red *kufiyyas*. And pockets stuffed with bullets and hand grenades.

A military jeep passed on the road below the hill, and they hid behind some rocks until it had disappeared. They went on walking, then stopped and took up their ambush positions. Soon, far off in the valley, the lights of the buses could be seen twinkling on the road beneath. Inside, the workers rested their heads on each other's shoulders, taking snatches of broken sleep. As the first bus came near,

Abu al-Raad shouted, 'Fire!'

Bullets flew. A bomb exploded near the bus and shrapnel scattered in every direction. The tyres blew. The bus spun, the workers screamed. A man threw open the door of the bus and flung himself to the ground. Others jumped out after him. Zuhdi found himself lying in a ditch with a piece of shrapnel in his shoulder.

'Fire!' yelled Usama. 'Fire on the second bus!'

More bullets. Fragments flew off rocks and the tyres of the second bus exploded. The other buses, which had stopped some distance away, now turned and headed back to the east.

The men ran through the darkness, hiding wherever they could find shelter, in holes, behind rocks and trees. There were several minor injuries, and two men lay motionless on the ground.

Zuhdi screamed, 'You bastards! We'll get you for this! You eat your own flesh! God damn you all! You, Usama! I know it's you! You pimp! You don't know anything. You just don't know! If I ever get my hands on you!'

When the firing stopped, Zuhdi stood and began walking towards the attackers bent forward, his hands on his head, 'I'll get you, Usama! I'll break your head open just like Shlomo's!'

Stealthily, like a thief, he climbed over the rocks. Usama was shouting, 'Pull back! Military vehicles! The Jews!'

The voice confirmed Zuhdi's suspicions. 'Usama! It *is* you, Usama! You bastard! What about your own cousin? And Abu Sabir? And me?' He stood on a rock and yelled, 'Usama! I knew it was you, Usama!'

Usama turned, amazed and shocked. It was Zuhdi! And Adil was probably with him! Well, too bad; they'd all be martyrs to the land, to the cause. He went on giving orders and the men continued to withdraw.

By now army trucks had halted on the road and soldiers with machine-guns jumped down. Searchlights cut through the darkness and loudspeakers blared: 'Give yourselves up! Surrender!'

The guerrillas continued to pull back and sheltered behind some rocks. Flares went off and again the loud-speakers called for surrender. The soldiers began to fan out and surround the area. Zuhdi crouched close to a rock, not knowing what to do next. Now you've had it, Zuhdi, by God. You're caught between two fires. You've had it. Machine-gun fire, hand grenades. He could hear the radio in the army trucks calling for reinforcements.

Bullets were flying directly above his head; one of the soldiers was firing his machine-gun regularly and pre-cisely. In the searchlight a guerrilla leaped in the air, then fell to the ground in a heap. Zuhdi, terrified, crouched closer to the rock. The machine-gun was still firing steadily above his head, the rat-tat-tat pounding mercilessly in his ears. If only I could get him! But he'd kill me first. A screwdriver's no match for a machine-gun. The guy's directly above your head, Zuhdi. Right above your head!

The guerrillas were retreating further and the soldier above Zuhdi leaped forward to follow them. He was in front of Zuhdi now, no more than an arm's length away. Stretch out your arm! Now! Grip the screwdriver tight. Yes, a screwdriver can match a machine-gun. But use it skilfully, as the Adil in prison said. Skilfully! Now!

He hurled himself at the soldier, who screamed and fell on his face. Bullets flew, bombs exploded, the machine-guns chattered. Still gripping the screwdriver he'd plunged into the man, Zuhdi crawled forward over the body. He shivered all over. 'There is no power, no strength but in God,' he thought. You've killed a man, Zuhdi! So what? You'd let Usama and the guerrillas be attacked over your head and you do nothing? You're a *shawka* now, a 'thorn'. Yes, a *shawka* in spite of yourself and everything. Well then. Pick up the machine-gun and fire! Fire!

Another soldier fell against a rock; the grenade he'd been carrying exploded. Bits of human flesh and khaki clothing went flying. Zuhdi crouched down again, close to the rock, feeling his own body all over. Nothing new. Just the shrapnel in his shoulder, nothing else.

God protect you, Saadiyya! Hamada's still so young. It would be easier if he were Sabir's age. Despite the cool breeze, he was dripping with sweat. Hooray for the sandstorms of Kuwait! Do you believe me, Adil al-Karmi, my brother? I swear by all that's holy that sitting in the Humuz Café's worth more than the whole world. *Aravim! Muloukhlakhim!* And still Adil al-Karmi keeps intervening to try to solve the Middle East conflict! While the screwdrivers and the wrenches fly, and bits of wood fall out of the sky. I'm not Christ, by God! And there's Shlomo, with his head split open. Poor guy. The man wasn't all bad. Just an ordinary man like me, like you too, Usama, you bastard! But Shlomo was also an ass. We were both asses, fighting over a bunch of clover and a factory-made pack-saddle. Fire! Fire!

Shrapnel flew through the air. Usama fell, his stomach split open, his entrails spilling out. He reached out his hand to touch the earth, mixed now with blood and tears. The land! Blood. Poetry. Dreams of love. In the village below the flute reminded you of weddings yet to come. A tendency to waywardness and madness in the heart. Brightly coloured scarves. Hands clasped, feet tapping the ground and sending the spirit high as seventh heaven. Mother! Adil! Nuwar! Tears veiling the vision. The organizations are afflicted with short-sightedness. Not true, you fool! But you don't know how a man feels when a plane flings him from an Arab airport to Lisbon. Pyjamas with a jacket on top. The airports of the world spit you out, and your own land receives you back. You cross the bridge and you hear her scream: 'You swine!' You're bleeding, Usama. You're dying. But you're still breathing. Down there in the town square people are eating *kinafa* and smiling. Their ears are stopped up; they're made of dough or clay. And Shahada, that bastard, showing off a gold ring bigger than his head. He smokes a pipe, Shahada, and laughs out of the corner of his mouth like a big foreign filmstar. The pimp's forgotten the land, forgotten his country, but remembered his hatred. And Adil, let him die a martyr to the homeland, to the cause. Zuhdi's following me like the ghost in *Hamlet*. He got out of prison only to meet his death. Where is he? I wish I could see him. I'd tell him to greet my mother for me. He was on that rock. He was screaming, 'Usama, I knew it was you!' What's happened to him?

Okay, thought Zuhdi, fire, just keep firing! You've become a *shawka* in spite of everybody. Oh Adil al-Karmi, God's peace be with you! I place Saadiyya and the children in your charge. Saadiyya. The Woman's Hour programme. Lentils have become food for the rich only. Abu Sabir's still going the rounds of the courts seeking his rights. How the sweat pours down. My tongue's so dry, like a piece of wood. Oh for a cup of tea! Let's see: two buckets and a broomstick, the TV screens. The Syrian and the mulberry tree, and his little boy Nidal. Yes, the whole struggle of the oppressed. Nidal ran across the prison yard and the prisoners wept. The guards did too. Tea. Two buckets, TV screens. Um Salim must be in her kitchen. And the white calf that gave you its life. But keep firing!

'Who's there?' he cried. 'Usama? What's happened? The searchlights. Your stomach's ripped open!'

'Send greetings to my mother, Zuhdi!'

'Me, greet your mother? Who's going to live to greet your mother? Let these bullets be a greeting for Usama's mother! Here, give me your grenade. Grenade, say hello to Saadiyya and the kids for me! Aah! Those bastards have just shot the head off one of your comrades!'

'Say hello to my mother . . . and Nuwar . . .'

'Please, friend, be quiet. Don't break my heart. You've got a terrible wound. You're dead. And so am I. Usama, you fool. You see this shoulder wound? . . . You can't see. Then touch it. Give me your hand. Can you feel it? That's shrapnel I got from you and your men. And now here I am at your side. Right here. I'm guarding you, Usama, despite your ripped stomach. Your wound's terrible. When the grenades flash and I see it, I want to throw up. Look, did you see? I've killed another one.'

A bullet grazed the side of his head and Zuhdi felt his ear fearfully. Terror. Rage. Frenzy. Madness. He stood up to his full height and yelled, 'You bastards! You filthy, rotten bastards!'

A burst of fire erupted from an American-made machine-gun. Oil money! So much for Arab unity!

Zuhdi, Zuhdi, my brother! Zuhdi's dead! And I'm dying too. There's no escape from death. You, mother, you're an angel. And me, I'm a real lion, mother; tell everyone I died a martyr, a martyr to the cause. A martyr to the land. I love you, mother. The oven fire. The smell of burning dung. The flute. Scarves. Wedding celebrations. The bride. Nuwar. Salih. Weddings. Yet to come . . .

Basil raced up the staircase to the upper floor of the house. He went into one of the bedrooms, opened a cupboard, took out a pile of papers – lists and leaflets – and then ran downstairs. As usual, Nuwar was sitting in the courtyard beside the fountain, oblivious of the world around her, engrossed in her letters. Basil tiptoed towards the passage which led to the entrance to the vault, careful to avoid being seen by his sister. He opened the wall and went inside. In a few minutes, he re-emerged, without the papers he'd been carrying.

He went up to Nuwar and sat beside her on a small chair, without saying a word. She was surprised: Basil wasn't usually so quiet. She contemplated his silhouette in the fading light of the coming dusk. 'What's wrong?' she asked.

'They've arrested Lina,' he replied calmly.

She gasped. 'Are you sure it's really her?'

'Absolutely. I was in the shop a few minutes ago and Hani told me. They got her out of bed in the middle of the night after barricading the whole street.'

Heavy silence. Nuwar imagined the torture her friend would be put through, while Basil wondered about the consequences of her arrest. What if Lina confesses? What if they discover that we're all in contact with Usama and his comrades? Now Lina's in prison, it'll be my turn next, for sure. Then they'll blow up the house. The family will be dispersed; that's what usually happens to people whose homes are demolished.

'Do you really believe Lina's enlisted?' Nuwar asked.

Basil shrugged, as though he didn't care. 'How should I know?' he said.

Nuwar glanced anxiously at her letter and Basil went on, 'There's no reason to hide the news from Salih.'

The mention of Salih's name surprised her.

'You think I don't know about the two of you?' Basil went on boldly. 'Everyone else knows, so why shouldn't I? There aren't any secrets in this town.'

She bowed her head but said nothing. Basil changed his tone. 'Now Salih,' he said encouragingly, 'there's a real man for you. There's someone worth making sacrifices for. But are you going to go on writing to him and visiting him in spite of what might happen?'

Nuwar still said nothing.

'Now if I were you,' Basil went on frankly, 'I wouldn't have kept the whole thing a secret. It's not a secret anyway. Everyone knows except Mother and Father.'

'Adil knows too?' she asked anxiously.

He smiled and gestured expansively, implying that there was no doubt that Adil knew.

'But what if Father finds out?' she whispered fearfully.

'Well, so what if he does? Why shouldn't he know? Why should you always be on the defensive? And what if some "good prospect" came along and asked to marry you and father agreed without discussing it with you?'

'Well,' she replied hesitantly, 'I'd refuse.'

'But what if Father agreed despite your refusal?'

'I'd go on saying no.'

'Even if Father had already agreed? The day's coming, Nuwar, when he'll insist on making a profitable match. Then you'll be forced to face the situation. You'll either have to accept it or tell him the truth about your relationship with Salih.'

'I can fend off any suitor without having to battle with

187

Father,' she replied disdainfully.

After a moment's silence, she continued: 'I'll talk about the money side of the thing, the fact that after I graduate I'll be able to work and help with the family expenses. That'll persuade them.'

'Yes, but what if the marriage contract that's offered is also a good one? What if the suitor's offer is more generous than yours? Suppose the man agreed that you could go on working even once you're married, so as to provide for Father?'

'That's most unlikely.'

'I don't agree. Many girls are doing that these days, so why shouldn't you? And I don't think Father wants a daughter of marriageable age to wait for ever.'

'So?'

'So you've got to tell him about Salih. Just say "I want Salih and no one else." '

'Are you crazy? Think what he'd say! What he'd do! You want me to be the cause of his death?'

He laughed nervously: 'Ah, you're all cowards, all of you. You, Adil, my mother, everyone. You use Father's illness as an excuse to avoid facing facts. Adil's been working in Israel for months without telling Father. Everyone knows, including Mother, but they're all like ostriches, hiding their heads in the sand and pretending that there's no storm going on around them. And you love Salih but won't admit it openly. Grandma's making plans for you to marry Usama; if he hadn't disappeared, she'd have talked to Father about it, and there'd have been no question of your agreeing or disagreeing. And Auntie thinks you want her son and has no doubt made a thousand and one plans for the wedding already. She probably thinks you're in love with Usama. All this going on, plus an expected suitor, and you still haven't taken one positive step. You act as though the whole thing didn't concern you.'

'Well, what should I do?'

'Tell Father frankly what you intend to do.'

'I can't.'

'You're a coward. You have to tell him before it's too late.'

'I can't.'

'You must. And quickly. Just between you and me, I smell a suitor in the wind.'

'What?'

'Yes. I heard a whisper. So be warned. Do you see what I'm getting at? If only you were more courageous now, you'd spare yourself a lot of problems later.'

'And what about you?'

'Me?'

'Don't you have any problems or secrets?'

'Don't I just! Lots of them!'

He smiled proudly. It pleased him to surround himself with an air of mystery and to excite his sister's curiosity. 'You mustn't compare your secrets with mine,' he said.

'Secrets, eh?'

'Oh yes . . . Important ones. But don't . . . I don't want to make you curious. No, I'm more interested in your problems. Not that I don't have my own secrets, very important ones too.'

He realized that he'd said too much, but the darkness hid his blushes. His mind returned to the main problem of the moment: Lina's arrest. He fell silent, and his ears strained to detect any unusual sound, anything that might take him by surprise. What would he do if the Jews came for him? What if Lina confessed? Under torture. Usama. The vault. The boxes. The pamphlets. What should he do? Lina was a strong, tough person, or so he'd been told, and she might well stand up to the torture. But could he do so himself? He made a quick decision. He'd run away and join Usama and his men.

'But what would I gain,' Nuwar was asking, 'by telling father about Salih now? He'd make my life hell. He might even have a stroke that'd finish him off.'

She went on and on but Basil wasn't listening. He was

making his escape plans. When I hear their cars coming, I'll go up on the roof, then I'll jump over the gutters to the neighbour's house. The roofs are only a few feet apart. Then I can run across the roofs to get out of the neighbourhood.

Nuwar was trying hard to attract his attention. 'What's the matter, Basil? Aren't you listening to me?'

'Sure, yes, I'm listening,' he replied distractedly. 'I just pray everything's going to be all right.'

Distraction. Anxiety. Lina. The Jews. Torture . . . Get a grip on yourself, Abu al-Izz, or you're done for. And the rest of the group, too, and the boxes; it'll be a disaster.

Footsteps sounded on the stairs, his ears strained in apprehension.

'It's Adil,' Nuwar announced.

His breathing slowed; his anxiety died down. Adil came up to them.

'Didn't you go . . . to work?' Nuwar asked him.

She was too embarrassed to mention the factory, though he knew that she knew. Just as she knew that he knew that she knew. But neither of them dared to bring up the subject openly.

'I went to Haifa with Abu Sabir,' he replied grimly.

'About an hour ago, some workers came by asking for you,' she said in some embarrassment.

'I know,' he muttered.

He turned and walked into the house. In the square he'd heard about the commando attack on the workers' buses. There'd been a battle in the Deir Sharaf region. Several workers had been injured, some guerrillas martyred and some Israeli soldiers killed. No one knew the details. He went upstairs. Nuwar and Basil followed him in silence.

He said hello to his mother as she hurried towards his father's room, then he flung himself down in a leather armchair and lit a cigarette. So you live on, Adil al-Karmi, with all your worries. If it weren't for Abu Sabir's case, you'd be in hospital by now, or a corpse laid out somewhere in a hole in the ground. I wish! It would have been a relief. Life has no purpose any more. What a life!

His father was bellowing for Basil, who reluctantly went into his bedroom. Another shout, this time for his wife. She left what she was doing in the kitchen and went in to him.

'Who's been playing with my kidney machine?' Abu Adil was shouting. 'You're always tampering with my things. No one stops the little ones coming in. One day they'll break this machine and nobody will lift a finger to stop them. I know what you want. You want to do away with me, so you'll all be rid of me.'

Basil came out, cursing to himself. He stood in front of Adil. 'When will God take him,' he asked, 'so we can have some peace?'

Adil frowned and puffed on his cigarette. When will God take me, he thought, so I can get some peace from everything? The guerrillas. The workers' buses. Death. Decline and fall. That's the worst problem. And Zuhdi? What's happened to Zuhdi? He must have become a *shawka*. He was on the bus that overturned in the ditch. Why did that have to happen? Why?

His father was now calling for his glasses and demanding to see Nuwar; she hurried into his room. A few minutes later she emerged, her father still ranting and cursing volubly. 'This place is like a cheap hotel,' he complained. 'Nothing's kept in order. Nothing's kept clean! Nothing's comfortable! And you! What do you all do? Nothing! Nothing!'

Nuwar stood before Adil and gestured towards her father's room. 'And what does he do, may I ask,' she said bitterly, 'except make our lives hell?'

Adil's head swam. How he wished his father would stop this constant complaining and leave everyone in peace. But he was still on the rampage, making his wife come and go, calling Basil, who went into the room again and left cursing. Adil felt as though his head was swelling up, like a boil about to burst. Nuwar came over to him. 'What's new in the world, Adil?' she asked gently.

New in the world? New? What world? Leave me alone in my misery, little sister. There's nothing new. No, everything's new. The wound's still there and it grows larger every day. There's Usama. Abu Sabir. Zuhdi. The buses. Zuhdi's a *shawka*. But I don't know who I am. I'm not a rose and I'm not a thorn. I'm nothing despite all my efforts to repair what the past has damaged. The situation has become too critical for any reform to work. Change is needed. Radical transformation. And probably in me, too.

Nuwar was saying, 'Have you heard the latest news?'

He gazed sadly at her childlike face. A wretched generation, my sister's, like the generations before it and those still to come. Misery spared no one.

'Lina's been arrested,' she said.

Astonishment! That's all I need. Young girls get sent to prison while I go on sitting here in this armchair: In a few minutes I'll sit down at the table, eat like everyone else, drink tea and smile. Then I'll go to sleep.

He heard his mother's voice: 'Dinner's ready.'

The mood around the family dinner table was silent, even grim. Abu Adil kept up his barrage of criticism. Suddenly he peered at Nuwar and announced, 'A suitor came to call today.'

'What?' Nuwar stopped eating.

Adil looked up from his plate at his father's face, but he said nothing. Basil suppressed a giggle and watched Nuwar with gloating excitement.

Their father continued calmly: 'Yes. It was Dr Izzat Abdu Rabbuh.'

He turned to Adil. 'You know him, of course?'

Adil shook his head and went on eating. Whether I know him or not, why bring me into it? You're the absolute master here, I'm just the family milch cow. Let the girl defend her rights. Let her learn how to face issues squarely. But she's weak and spineless. All that the girls of this country know of revolution is what they read in books. But then, there's Lina and the others like her. Why can't my sister be like Lina? But how can I ask her to be like Lina when I don't ask myself to be like Salih? This decrepit house of ours produces nothing but illness and cowardice.

His eyes met Basil's sarcastic gaze. And you, Basil? What about you? Are you like us? I haven't heard you boasting lately about your heroic battles in prison. What's happened? Have you forgotten how you wrung the military governor's neck, my young brother?

The two brothers smiled affectionately at each other; tenderness welled up in Adil's heart and he felt a deep sense of sorrow.

Abu Adil glanced at each member of the family in turn. 'Well, what's wrong with everyone?' he demanded. 'Why are you all so quiet? Don't you know Dr Izzat? He's a cultivated young man from a most respectable family. His financial situation is exceptional. He's clever, too; although he only graduated two years ago, he knows how to generate business. Patients gather like flies around his surgery.'

'A very successful fellow indeed!' commented Basil.

'Yes, and he's coming to see you tomorrow,' the father informed Nuwar.

Adil's expression showed his disgust, but he didn't comment. He just went on eating. I wish the girl would defend her dignity, he thought. If she doesn't, she's not worthy of respect. Let her become just one more traditional Arab woman; I'll have no pity for her.

'Say something,' Basil whispered encouragingly to Nuwar. 'Speak up!'

Nuwar was having trouble eating. She nudged him in the ribs and whispered, 'Shut up!'

Looking over at his wife, Abu Adil said, 'Teach this girl how to behave in front of the man.'

Um Adil shook her head, but made no reply.

Nuwar now spoke: 'But I don't even know him!'

'Of course not; did you expect to?' her father replied. Then he turned to Adil and added gravely, 'Dr Izzat has a very positive attitude that does him credit; he said he would agree to Nuwar's working after she graduates, so that she can use her salary to help with some of the problems in this house.'

Adil glared. 'I'm quite capable of fulfilling the family responsibilities if Nuwar really wants to get married,' he said contemptuously.

He stared hard at his sister, silently urging her to face up to the situation. But she deliberately avoided his gaze. Her heart was pounding, but, she thought, what good would it do to argue with her father? He might suffer some kind of fatal attack; why take chances? Peaceful means were more likely to be effective. Better simply to behave badly before the suitor so he'd change his mind.

Her grandmother interrupted: 'But is it appropriate for Nuwar to become engaged under the present circumstances?' she asked tremulously.

'What do you mean?' frowned Abu Adil.

She folded her hands in her lap, in a gesture of total submission, but whispered, 'What about Usama?'

The smile on Basil's face broadened and he cleared his throat meaningfully. 'Nuwar, will you please pass the salt?' he asked.

She handed him the salt, banging it down angrily on the table. 'Okay. I get it,' she whispered.

'Well, what about Usama?' persisted her grandmother.

'What's Usama got to do with it?' her father demanded.

The old lady looked from Adil to Basil to Nuwar, but none of them took the hint and pursued the issue. But one of the younger children asked, 'Where's Usama? Has he come back yet?'

'Be quiet, child,' Abu Adil said gruffly. 'Eat your dinner.'

The child turned to his mother and whispered, 'What's wrong with Usama, Mama?'

'I don't know. Hurry up and finish your meal.'

With admirable courage, the grandmother persisted: 'But only a month ago Zakiyya had her heart set on engaging Nuwar to Usama.'

Abu Adil stared at his mother, who was by now clearly agitated. 'What are you saying, Mother?' he said coldly. 'You mean I should marry my daughter to a young man who's disappeared? Have you forgotten that he's charged with murdering an officer? Have you forgotten that he's a fugitive from justice, and the Israeli security forces are looking for him?'

'Usama's no fugitive from justice!' cried Basil angrily.

The boy's father smiled derisively as he gazed at his son. 'Ah, Basil,' he said. 'No doubt you admire Usama, don't you? No doubt your puerile imagination has made quite a hero of him; you probably dream of doing what he's done. Who knows? I may have some such surprises in store for me. These days no home's safe from such things. A great many boys are giving their parents headaches. But watch your step, son; this isn't a game, you're not acting in some TV serial. You're not James Bond – or maybe you are, and I don't know it.'

Basil was staring at his father in hatred and defiance. Noticing his expression, Abu Adil shouted at the family, 'You see how this prodigal brat looks at me? Lower your eyes, boy, don't you dare give me those insolent stares. This whole generation's rotten. God curse all who planted their seed!'

Basil spoke up defiantly. 'Usama's not a fugitive from justice,' he said, 'and for one good reason – there's no justice whatsoever in this country.'

'Well, well, well!' snickered his father, 'the boy's got a tongue – he talks! So that's it, eh? No justice, eh? How bright you are! Where did you get such genius, boy?'

'I'm my father's son,' Basil answered quickly.

'Get out of here,' stormed his father. 'Get out of my sight!'

'But I'm hungry and I want to finish my dinner,' replied Basil stubbornly.

'Get out of my sight! Nothing to eat for you!'

Adil tried to lighten the atmosphere. 'Let him finish eating, Father, please. Punish him if you want, but not this way. He's thin enough as it is. He needs his food.'

He smiled at his father and at Basil and went on: 'And remember he's got exams coming up. I hope the results this year will do us all credit, Basil.'

Their father gave in, grumbling. 'The boy's been insolent ever since he went to prison,' he said. 'He learned his bad manners there. I'm not responsible for whatever mess he gets himself into. I'm not responsible for whatever problems he may cause us. But listen and listen carefully Basil. When you're sitting at my table you must behave and speak politely. Do you understand?'

Basil didn't bother to reply. He was busy thinking, and his thoughts frightened him. What if the Jews found out about the secret vault? Well, let them! I hope they discover it and blow this whole house up over your heads. You're all cowards. You're worthless, the lot of you. I'm taking off. I'll join the so-called 'fugitives from justice' like Usama.

There was a moment's silence.

'Dr Izzat's coming tomorrow afternoon,' announced Abu Adil, 'and I want you all to be present. You'll be here, Adil, won't you?' he asked politely.

'No, I'm afraid not,' answered Adil, a bit too nonchalantly. 'I'm extremely busy these days.'

'Ah yes, how are things at the farm?' asked his father, feigning genuine interest.

Adil shook his head slightly, looked down into his cup of tea, and said nothing. Their grandmother spoke up again, her voice weak and trembling: 'Oh, Zakiyya will be so hurt! It's not right for Nuwar to become engaged to a strange man when one of her cousins wants her.'

Abu Adil smiled at his mother: 'One of her cousins, that's your own daughter's son, you mean. Well, let's not argue, Mother. You know I respect family relationships. But I simply will not marry my daughter to . . .'

He stopped, glanced piercingly at Basil and finished: '. . . to a fugitive fom justice.'

'Usama's not a fugitive from justice,' insisted Basil. 'Usama's more honourable than the rest of us put together.'

He got up trembling, his eyes bulging, crumbs of food spilling from the corners of his mouth. 'I've had enough,' he said, almost hysterically. 'Go on, all of you, eat until you burst. Eat till you get indigestion. Eat till your bellies swell and you've grown double chins. But just remember that at

197

this moment Usama's probaby hungry. Honourable men are always hungry.'

His father had begun to breathe hard and was clearly furious. Adil said angrily, 'Look, Basil, if you've had enough, just let everyone else finish. Why don't you go to your room and get on with some studying? I'll come up and talk to you after dinner.'

Basil moved towards the hall while Adil tried to pacify his father. 'Please, Father,' he pleaded, 'don't blame him. Remember who Usama is.'

Basil stopped in his tracks and turned back towards the dinner table. 'I'm not defending Usama's conduct because he's my cousin, and yours too,' he said angrily. 'Family ties mean nothing to me and the proof is that I won't defend *your* behaviour.'

Adil looked at his brother sadly, then tried to hide his feelings by looking down into his teacup, his heart pounding. My whole life's just one blow after another, he thought. Basil knows, Nuwar knows, my mother knows, but no one dares to admit the truth, no one wants to say it to my face. Oh, much revered father! Your sickness is being transmitted to all of us.

The sound of a car door being slammed in the street outside reached Basil. He peered through the window trying to see the entrance to the house, his heart beating rapidly. He went up to the roof, walked to the edge and looked down. The street was dark and quiet. He couldn't see anyone in front of the house. Next door, the neighbour locked the door of his truck, then walked to the back and began unloading crates of vegetables, carrying them to the one shop in the street where lights still blazed. Basil went down to his room and stood by the window, watching the front of the house. He was frightened . . . Can I stand the torture? I'm not sure. The best thing was to run. He went back to the roof and tried to gauge the distance to the next roof. Not too far, a couple of feet, perhaps. I can easily step across that.

In his room he paced up and down nervously. He couldn't stand being alone much longer. The interminable waiting for the arrival of the soldiers – even though they were nowhere in sight. He was upset, but also lonely, very lonely. He went back down to the dining room and stood watching his family, still sitting at the table eating. Suddenly he felt he hated them all, and tears froze in his eyes as he looked from one person to the next. I hate my father because he personifies sickness. I hate my mother because she's the personification of submissiveness. I hate my old grandmother: she represents man's collapse in the face of time. And Nuwar's hateful because she's spineless. She's unsuited to her role in life. As for Adil, I scorn Adil because he's not like Salih or Usama. The children mean nothing to me. I'm a stranger in this house, damn this house!

Then, without warning, he heard himself speaking solemnly. Slowly. As though reading a formal statement, he said, 'Nuwar al-Karmi loves Salih al-Safadi, but won't admit it. She's promised to wait for him as long as he's in prison. That's assuming the occupation continues, of course. If the occupation ends, she plans to marry him no matter what all of you say. And most of all, no matter what her father says.'

Nuwar moaned, from the depths of her soul. 'Basil . . .' she cried out in anguish.

But her brother merely looked back at her steadily and continued: 'Nuwar al-Karmi loves Salih al-Safadi and will marry no one else. But she's a coward. Too much of a coward to stand up to other people.'

His father sat there motionless, his knife and fork in the air. Adil put his elbows on the table and rested his head in his hands, shocked at Basil's words. His mind raced ahead. He may well spill the beans about me next, he thought. Yes, he might just do it. Who'd have expected this? What's wrong with the boy? Has he gone mad?

'Nuwar al-Karmi,' Basil repeated in the tone of a radio announcer, 'loves Salih al-Safadi; she writes letters to him and receives letters back. She visits him in prison and pretends to the authorities that she's his fiancée.'

The knife and fork now fell from Abu Adil's grip and his head dropped forward.

'Basil! Basil!' Nuwar screamed.

His mother joined in: 'Basil, dear boy, what's come over you?'

The young man walked on into the room, stopped directly behind Nuwar's chair and repeated his news bulletin: 'Nuwar al-Karmi loves Salih al-Safadi; she writes to him and visits him in prison.'

'Is this true?' asked their father, his voice hoarse. 'Is what the boy says true?'

No one answered. Adil went on listening, transfixed as Basil repeated once more: 'Nuwar al-Karmi loves Salih al-Safadi and will marry no one else. Nuwar al-Karmi loves a freedom fighter. But I don't know how any freedom fighter could love a spineless girl like Nuwar al-Karmi.'

Hiding her face in her hands, Nuwar wept. 'That's enough, Basil,' she said through her tears. 'Please, that's enough. Be quiet, God damn you! What have I ever done to you that you should hurt me so much?'

Her father stared at her in amazement. 'So it's true, then?' he muttered.

'One hundred per cent true,' answered Basil indifferently.

Nuwar jumped to her feet and burst out, 'Yes, yes! I *will* marry him! I won't marry anyone but Salih. No one else. Not Abdu Rabbuh or anyone else. I'll never marry anyone except Salih, even if I have to wait a hundred years. I'll only marry Salih.'

Beads of perspiration broke out on their father's forehead and he gasped for breath. He gripped Adil's arm. 'She visits him in public?' he gasped. 'What must people be saying about the venerable house of al-Karmi, and about me?'

His wife began to sob. 'You'll have to account to God for

what you've done, Basil,' she cried plaintively. 'Have you lost your mind? I'm ruined, finished. It's not enough that one of my sons has gone mad, it looks like I'm going to lose his father too!'

She continued bemoaning her ill luck, while Nuwar ran out of the room.

Adil turned to Basil. 'Well, are you satisfied?' he demanded.

'No, not yet,' his brother replied calmly. 'Not till I expose you too!'

Adil looked down. What else could happen? he thought wildly. Oh confusion, oh my speechless heart, where will the next blow come from?

In the same news announcer's voice, Basil intoned, 'Adil al-Karmi's been working in Israel for several months as a common labourer. When the men left the farm, he abandoned it and got a job in an Israeli factory.'

The father's hand clasped the table convulsively. 'Call the doctor,' he gasped, 'or take me to hospital.'

His head fell forward and hit the table with a bang. Adil rushed to phone for a taxi. He lifted his father and tried to help him into the living room. While they were struggling through the hall, a loud banging sounded on the door below: 'Open up! Open up!' soldiers were shouting. 'Open the door!'

Basil raced for the roof. When he looked down he could see that security vehicles had already blocked off the road and yellow searchlights were flashing all over the neighbours' houses. He stood on the edge of the roof of his house, looked far down below, took a deep breath and jumped. As he disappeared into the darkness, the soldiers were already beating their rifle butts against the door below.

Abu Adil was in the hospital. Meanwhile every room, every corner, of the house was being searched. Electronic metal detectors were beeping constantly. The soldiers came to a stop in front of the basement wall and broke through it with their pickaxes. It took them half an hour to get into the vault and remove the boxes. Adil and Nuwar were arrested. They were released after two days of non-stop interrogation. On the third day the family received an order to vacate the house.

Men had gathered in the nearby streets, whispering about the impending destruction of the Karmi house, about the arms cache found in the vault, about Basil, Usama, Lina and their secret guerrilla cell. The women assembled on the roof-tops, watching all the family's belongings being moved out of the house at frenzied speed. There was only half an hour left. Beds, sofas, refrigerator, washing machine. Everything they could carry. Abu Nawwaf, Shahada and Sabir hadn't gone to the factory that day. They helped Adil move the furniture. No one referred to Zuhdi's death. Abu Sabir, a constant flow of tears streaming down his face, stood at the end of the street watching the men move in and out of the doomed house. Um Sabir stood on a neighbour's roof, beating her hands together in distress. From a window of Usama's mother's house, Adil's mother watched the household belongings she knew so well taken out of their accustomed places for ever.

'Tell Adil not to forget the kidney machine,' she shouted to Sabir.

Sabir nodded and went over to tell Adil what his mother had said.

'Yes, okay. Thanks, Sabir,' answered Adil. 'Now go and help Shahada with the rest of the stuff.'

Nuwar was still in her room, stuffing clothes into a row of suitcases by the door. A soldier watched her every movement while she packed.

Abu Nawwaf approached Adil. 'Your mother says don't forget the kidney machine,' he whispered. 'Okay?'

'Yes, all right. Here, give Abu Badawi a hand with the gas stove, don't let him carry it by himself.'

Adil found that he instinctively rejected all thoughts of saving the kidney machine. Whenever the thought crossed his mind, he pushed it away . . . Carry this . . . carry that . . . careful down the steps. Don't trip and bang your head. No, no! Not like that. Turn the metal frame of the bed around; it won't go through the door that way. Put the cups in the vegetable crate like this, and the plates too. Careful! Subhi, give him a hand with the boxes. Here, I'll help . . . No, don't bother with those sofas, just take the leather ones. We only need useful things, leave the rest of the stuff to be blown up with the house. Necessities only! Necessities! Nuwar, please now, only the clothes you really need, okay? What? No more empty suitcases? Never mind, bundle them up in sheets . . . Shahada, please help her. You're right, my friend, people have to help each other; how else could we survive?

'Ten more minutes,' a soldier shouted.

The kidney machine. He pushed the thought away, and began to walk up and down the stairs to keep his mind and body occupied . . . I won't take that damned machine. Yes, I will. No, I won't. Yes, I will.

'Hey, Adil, give him a hand or that big wardrobe'll topple over!'

As though the Lord himself had summoned him, Adil

ran to grab hold of the wardrobe, putting himself beneath its weight and trying to empty his mind. The wardrobe seemed to weigh a ton. He felt the sweat break out on his body with the effort; his shoulder-blades creaked beneath the load. Around him he could hear men shouting, 'Up, lift it up, up!'

'Time's up,' the soldier shouted. 'Come on now, time's up! No, I'm sorry, you can't go back upstairs, sir. Down you go! Come on now!'

But what about the machine? His father's kidney machine! Should I tell the officer? He'd probably put off the demolition for a few minutes so we could get it out. But if I wanted to take it so much why didn't I move it out in the beginning? Adil, for God's sake, be decisive for once in your life! Emotions won't help you. Would you kill a man then? Kill your own father? But men are always being killed. And if my father goes on living, we'll all die . . . Me, Nuwar, the children. Haven't we lost enough already? Usama, Basil, the family estate. And all in self-defence. In defence of a dignified, honourable life. Let my father die! No, let him live! If you save him, you'll save your own soul from the damnation of a terrible crime.

He hurried over and touched the officer on the shoulder. As the man turned Adil stared at him in astonishment. That face! That man! You carried his daughter on your back! You stripped off his stars and carried his daughter. You carried a human being. And you felt your own sense of humanity swell and deepen as you became aware of the Israeli officer as a human being. Your father too, you've carried him for a long time. But when his existence becomes a threat to your own humanity . . . Now this officer . . . his face is like my father's. There's not much difference.

'Did you want something?' the Israeli asked.

Adil shook his head. 'When are you going to blow it up?' he asked.

'Now.'

He gazed at the house as though through a mist. For the last time. Never again, Adil, will you see the place where you were born. Those steps – how many times have you gone up and down them, on all fours, at a crawl, at a run? The big courtyard there, with its pool and marble basins. Long evenings spent beneath the lemon tree with friends and relatives. Evenings. Memories. Can a man forget his memories so easily? This sense of longing that binds one to the past. Chains. Chains of longing binding one to the past. Chains. Chains of silver and jasmine. But chains nonetheless.

A dusty easterly wind blew across the bridge. The men stood some distance away, sad-eyed, staring at the condemned house. What can a man feel other than sadness at the hour of sudden adversity? A hand gripped his arm, the mutilated hand of Abu Sabir.

Adil smiled bitterly. We're one in our grief. You've suffered a loss, and so have I. Both of us. But we can still hope that our children will succeed where we've failed. Don't shed tears, Abu Sabir. This house isn't worth a single one of your fingers.

'Adil, you deserve better than this,' murmured Abu Sabir, unable to control his tears.

'Don't cry, please Abu Sabir,' urged Adil, 'not for any injustice you think has been done to me. Which of us deserves what he gets in life? No, we mourn our fate, but the trust men place in us keeps us going and comforts us. Why do we weep? We've lost a lot, it's true. But we still have a great deal. Look at your son, Abu Sabir. He's grown like a palm tree – tall, deep-chested, broad-shouldered. And his eyes! Just look at those eyes of his! There are new horizons there, the unlimited horizons of tomorrow.'

'Adil,' said Abu Sabir, 'don't worry about this house. We'll build you a new one. I promise. We'll build it together. A house that can't be blown up.'

Then came the deafening sound of the explosion. The great house shuddered and stones seemed to fall from the sky. Then the traditional ululation of the women burst out; the sound of emotion, joy and sorrow filled the street.

Take a deep breath, Adil told himself. Tears. Dust. Fog. He could smell lemonwood through the acrid aroma of dust and crumbling stone. The lemon tree was burning in the rubble of the courtyard. The soldiers looked so arrogant in their dark cars. A thirst for revenge, for rebellion, stirred deep within him. I'm not cruel, but I'm filled with rage and bitterness, filled up to here. And these cowering crowds. And you yourself, Adil, a god of patience, that's what they say. What could be worse than admitting you're an impotent god, unable to assert your own rights or anyone else's? The process of ascent and fall goes on. A god-like ascent to the heights of Mount Aibal. And descent through seaweed into the gutters and decaying refuse. You search for yourself in other people's eyes, Adil. You find yourself mirrored in the eyes of the hungry, the naked, the homeless, those who live in tents. The winds and storms toss you in all directions. But the will to live still beats within you, defiant and instinctive. What can you do? Your spirit is bottled up; it can't find a way out. You experience sorrow, repress your emotions, and wait. Nevertheless! This mind of yours at least keeps you awake, wards off the drunkenness of indifference. Your heart rages and storms, yet the energy's suppressed by the machinery of oppression.

If only you knew how to begin! If only you were more cruel, or harder of heart, you'd blow up everything you could lay hands on, from the Atlantic to the Gulf and on to the world's furthest reaches. You'd leave no two stones standing. You'd uproot the trees, exposing the infections beneath the earth's surface to the light of the sun, to the breezes of spring. You'd turn everything upside-down. And begin again. Slowly, very slowly. Here a seedling. There a tree. Here a flower. And you, young Sabir, a tall, broad-shouldered palm. Your hands would bring rocks from the depths of the earth and from the mountains.

Those stones would shine like raw diamonds. We could

colour them, decorate them, and build them into rows of beautiful houses that would stretch as far as the eye could see and stand for all eternity. The soldiers' metal detectors could ring all they liked, we wouldn't hear them. We'd hear only the music of flutes in the meadows. Sheep would graze calmly in the golden fields of Ibn Amir plain, and peace would cover the world. Peace and joy. Peace would reign from the rocky heights of Mount Aibal to the pine forests of Jirzim.

The house lay in ruins. The men dispersed. The women came down from the roofs. Adil slipped away from the crowd, cutting through the narrow back streets and heading for the main square.

He stood on the pavement watching the people on their way home, on their way to work. They lived their everyday lives stoically, silently. Nothing had changed. The square stood where it always had; the town clock ticked slowly as it always had. Only the flowers seemed to have grown larger, taller; otherwise nothing had changed.

The smell of roasting coffee and *kinafa* reached him. The chimneys of the soap factory poured clouds of smoke over the ancient roofs of the houses. People were eating, shopping, smiling.

Adil walked through the square in silence, crossing the main street in the centre of town. The street peddlers were crying out their wares: 'Fish from Gaza!' 'Oranges from Jaffa!' 'Bananas from Jericho!'

The liquorice and carob-drink peddler clashed his cymbals rhythmically.

A newspaper boy passed by, crying: *'Al-Quds! Al-Shaab! Al-Fajr!* Kissinger announces solution to Middle East crisis!' Farid al-Atrash continued to lament the unhappy day of his birth. People went about their business, buying vegetables, fruit and bread.